IT IS FINISHED

Exposing the Conquered Giants of Fear, Pride, and Condemnation

Daniel T. Newton

Contributing authors and editors: Downing McDade, Katherine Marx, Eric Heinrichs, Austin Chappell, James Bell IV, Elizabeth Newton and the Grace Place Leadership Team

ISBN: 9781957601045

"So when Jesus had received the sour wine, He said, 'It is finished!' And bowing His head, He gave up His spirit."

—John 19:30

Resources By Daniel Newton and Grace Place Ministries:

Truth in Tension: 55 Days to Living in Balance
Immeasurable: Reviewing the Goodness of God
Never Give Up: The Supernatural Power of Christlike Endurance
The Lost Art of Discipleship
The Lost Art of Discipleship Workbook
The Lost Art of Perseverance
All Things
GP Music: Beginnings – Worship Album

For more information on these books
and other inspiring resources, visit us at
www.GracePlaceMedia.com

TABLE OF CONTENTS

Foreword

Words are powerful. Words are important. Words carry impartations, and they also release breakthroughs. When Jesus spoke the words, "it is finished," He really meant what He said. His words are truth. The book you hold in your hands contains many words intended to bring you into this truth. This book, filled with words, has the power to revolutionize your life, but in order for that to happen, you must first be willing to receive the power that it contains.

Over the years, I've had many conversations through email, social media, and personal messages with Daniel Newton. I've also been blessed on several occasions to spend time with him in person. Every interaction has been life-giving and filled with the truth of God's Word and the wonder of His glory because this is the realm in which Daniel has chosen to live. This glory fills every area of his life, and it overflows to those who are around him.

When I was ministering quite a few years ago in Spokane, Washington, Daniel brought a team from Grace Place Ministries to the meetings. The pure passion and zeal that these young people brought to the services was palpable. It was overflowing from their lives, for they had been soaked and saturated in the Word and Spirit, and it brought forth so much life! Their presence set the atmosphere for that entire weekend of meetings. Miracles happened, signs and wonders followed the preaching of the Word, and many people encountered Jesus Christ as the Lord of Glory. It's amazing what can happen when your mind has been renewed in such a way that the finished work of Jesus consumes every part of who you are—spirit, soul, and body. It's amazing what happens when you believe the right words.

Daniel Newton's new book, It Is Finished, contains the rich revelations he has received over many years as he sought God for the answers needed by the new believers in Christ whom he was discipling. What he learned and shared with them showed them how to live victoriously in the fullness of the price Jesus paid on The Cross of Calvary. As Daniel has so powerfully revealed in this book, a great many of the problems new believers face (all believers, really) are nothing more than wrong thoughts and concepts developed over many years, misguided traditions, and outright lies the enemy tells us in an attempt to hinder our progress. In far too many cases, it works. We get sidetracked with this "stuff" and fail to see the simplicity of the truth: that the price has been paid and our victory has been assured. All that remains to be done is for us to lay hold of what is already ours and start living in it.

In the very first chapter of this book, "Giants in the Promised Land," Daniel shows what the children of Israel, newly liberated from slavery in Egypt, faced as they finally entered their Promised Land. It was full of giants. For most of the spies sent in to assess the situation, this was totally discouraging, and they came away convinced that there was no way they could take the land. For Joshua and Caleb, however, the giants were mere challenges, and these two men came away assured, as

Caleb reported, "We are well able to take it" (Numbers 13:30). As Daniel so eloquently sums it up, "God has given you the truth you need to combat every giant in your Promised Land."

In this way, chapter after chapter, Daniel deals with the deceptive thinking that has hindered Christians of all generations and applies scriptural revelations that enables us to overcome that deceptive thinking. His goal is to help believers everywhere live a more free and productive life in Christ. Those who read the book and apply its concepts will indeed achieve that goal. This is a book I highly recommend, and I suggest that you not only study it for yourself. Pick up multiple copies of it and give them away, as a gift that will sow the seed of right revelation and produce a harvest of right living! Everything you need is found in the glory of God through the finished work of Christ. Truly, It Is Finished.

– Joshua Mills

Speaker and bestselling author, *Creative Glory* and *Power Portals*
International Glory Ministries
www.joshuamills.com

Introduction

When I think of Jesus' concept of discipleship, I don't think of mega-churches, massive choirs, and convenient Sunday school pamphlets. I think of something that's rough around the edges yet far more meaningful—something hands-on, fruitful, and life-giving. I think of something that requires sacrifice, commitment, and intentionality. I think of family...a family in all its glory with mistakes, messes, victories, and triumphs. I think of my normal, everyday life.

Over the past twenty years of ministry, I have discipled and fathered hundreds of men and women from around the world. With each individual, new challenges arise. Running a discipleship ministry with 18-30-year-olds has had its fair share of difficulties.

I often joke that ministry would be easy if people weren't involved. When it comes to people, there is no easy, step-by-step guide to life transformation. In fact, it is an ever-fluctuating process. Transformation is not immediate but comes from the gradual renewal of our minds according to Romans 12:2.

That being said, problems don't bother me. It's part of the journey. The people I'm pouring into are worth the process.

Without resistance, there's no growth. It's through mistakes that lessons are learned and new life emerges. The bigger question is never, "What's the problem?" but rather, "How do you handle the problem?"

When we are confronted with our weaknesses and shortcomings, we can either run and hide, pretending they're not there, or face them head-on. I encourage everyone I mentor to look their problems square in the eyes and conquer them with the truth. *What does God say about this? What truth from His Word relates to this situation?*

When personal issues or conflicts arise in those I disciple, I look for the root of the issue, so I can quickly address what is going on under the surface and confront it with God's Word. After years of doing this, I have noticed an interesting trend, a common thread over many scenarios. Each person may struggle differently, whether with negative mindsets, addictions, demonic spirits, or simple immaturity and irresponsibility. However, every issue almost always comes down to the same three roots:

Fear.
Pride.
Condemnation.

Now, before I continue, I want to be clear that I am not in any way proposing to have a simple formula to diagnose every problem. I'm presenting an observation I've found to be true as I disciple young adults. The root of nearly every negative behavior is fear, pride, or condemnation.

At its core, however, this is not a book about fear, pride, and condemnation at all. More important than understanding these three roots is understanding the power of the finished work of the Cross. In the heavenly realm, your victory is already secured. Through the channel of the Spirit within you, you receive the love that casts out fear, the humility that crushes pride, and the gift of righteousness that silences condemnation.

When we saturate our hearts and minds with these unchanging truths and connect with them intimately, we can truly step into the abundant life Christ purchased for us. He *already* paid the price to make us new creations and give us new identities in Him! Our behavior and lifestyle merely reflect what we believe. It is critical to understand that simple belief changes will result in true lifestyle changes.

The fruit of who we are is the product of an intricate root system within each of our hearts. "Even so, every good tree bears good fruit, but a bad tree bears bad fruit...Therefore by their fruits you will know them" (Matt. 7:17). In other words, our conduct reveals our beliefs. This is why I'm not afraid to ask those I disciple, "Why do you do what you do?" I look beneath the surface because I know change starts from within.

That's what this book is for. I want to convict your heart with truth and stir your spirit with the Word. I want you to come face to face with the victory that is already yours. It's one thing to know about it, but it's another thing entirely to make it your own and experience it daily.

I pray that as you read, you find encouragement and hope rising within you to overcome the three obstacles of fear, pride, and condemnation. While they may seem like giants, they are merely defeated foes attempting to rob you of the fulfilling life Jesus died to give you. I believe that by the end of this book, you will be staring these "giants" down, victoriously declaring, "For who is this uncircumcised Philistine, that he should defy the armies of the living God?" (1 Sam. 17:26). May God bless you with an abundance of grace as you learn to reign in this victorious life (see Rom. 5:17).

Chapter One

Giants in The Promised Land

When God brought His people out of Egypt, it wasn't a walk in the park. Moses led the children of Israel away from the tyranny of Pharaoh, shaking off the chains of 400 years of bondage, shame, and affliction. For the first time in centuries, the Israelites had the opportunity to leave their past of slavery behind and step into a new life. However, this new life wasn't quite what they were expecting...

There were giants in the Promised Land.

The very place God led His people was a land inhabited by their enemies. The inheritance they had been predestined to receive was crawling with adversity.

The book of Numbers recounts the murmuring that filled the camp as God's chosen people failed to see beyond their circumstances. They had been given a promise: a land flowing with milk and honey. Yet when they witnessed the land that awaited them, they measured themselves according to the size of the giants and not the size of God's promise. They were grasshoppers in their own sight.

"There we saw the giants (the descendants of Anak came from the giants); and we were like grasshoppers in our own sight, and so we were in their sight."
– Numbers 13:33

Only Joshua and Caleb were able to see higher, farther, and deeper. They couldn't care less about the giants in the land, knowing that the God of the universe was in their midst.

God gave Israel a promise: a land of victory. All they had to do was remain steadfast and possess it. It was already theirs. God had already declared it. So, why all the giants? Why was the land flowing with milk and honey also a land overtaken by beasts and enemies?

We can ask ourselves the same question today. *Why is this Christian life not everything I thought it would be? God has given me all of these promises, but why does it feel like there's so much opposition? Why are there so many giants in my life?*

Great questions.

We hang in the balance between facts and truth. Facts are what the world and our observations tell us. They can be subject to change. Truth, however, is permanent and absolute. It's the undying reality of who Christ is and what He's accomplished for us through His death and resurrection. Facts are giants, and the truth is a Promised Land.

When negative facts (addictions, sicknesses, overwhelming emotions, etc.) seem to overrun our lives, we must look higher. We shouldn't see ourselves as grasshoppers but as victorious children who have been given an everlasting hope. We must pick up our slingshots and take on the giants that so persistently wish to intimidate us.

So, what are these giants? What are we up against? What are the lies that come to rob us of truth?

Fear, pride, and condemnation.

I've seen repeatedly that virtually every issue that distracts us from the Promised Land of Christ's victory can be traced to one of these three roots. When you are faced with financial issues, fear comes creeping in. When your relationships are struggling and you can't admit your mistakes, there stands pride. When you can't get over what you did yesterday, last month, or twenty years ago, condemnation is on the scene.

These are obviously only a few scenarios of an infinite number of circumstances I could paint. Yet, I guarantee you that nearly every internal war you face is ultimately against one of these three foes.

These are the giants of your Promised Land. However, there's good news. The land is already yours. The victory is won. Everything you've ever needed for life and godliness has already been provided in the Son (see 2 Peter 1:3). Your victory is just as sure as the words that echoed from our Savior's lips when He hung on the tree of Calvary: "It is Finished" (see John 19:30).

God has given you the truth you need to combat every giant in your Promised Land. The truth comes to set you free. When you're faced with fear, the truth is unfailing love. When you're faced with pride, the truth is humility. When you're faced with condemnation, the truth is God's free gift of righteousness. Jesus *is* Truth. He modeled perfect love, perfect humility, and perfect righteousness. He is the solution. He is the stone that struck Goliath, and He is the stone that is waiting to strike every invading giant in your life. Christ in you is the promise-keeper, and a victorious life, right here, right now, is your inheritance. It's your Promised Land.

A Perspective that's Bigger than Giants

Joshua and Caleb's response set the perfect example for us to follow. "Then Caleb quieted the people before Moses, and said, 'Let us go up at once and take possession, for we are well able to overcome it'" (Num. 13:30). Caleb never lost sight of the promise. He remembered who God was to him: the God who split the sea, turned water to blood, and conquered the Egyptians. He knew the children of Israel were "well able to overcome!"

Do you believe this about yourself? Do you believe that, as a son or daughter of the King of Kings and Lord of Lords, you can and will overcome every obstacle and every giant that comes to disempower you? It starts with remembering who He is and what He's promised. The land is prepared for you, but is your heart prepared for the land? Are you convinced of the truth and victory of Jesus Christ? We should learn from the mistakes of the Israelites and never forget the God who redeemed us.

"How often they provoked Him in the wilderness, and grieved Him in the desert! Yes, again and again they tempted God, and limited the Holy One of Israel. They did not remember His power: the day when He redeemed them from the enemy..."
– Psalm 78:40-42

One of my spiritual fathers, Steve Backlund, says, "Your past is not your problem; your current beliefs are. Your problem is not your problem; your perspective is." My heart for you is that you would take your rightful place in God's Promised Land and see beyond your issues. I want you to identify all the giants trespassing in your life so you can replace them with the truth and freedom found only in Jesus.

As you unmask and unveil the lies that fight for dominion over your mind, they become targets for God's sufficient grace. God knows exactly what you're going through. Jesus experienced your problems long before you ever did. "For we do not have a High Priest who cannot sympathize with our weaknesses, but was in all points tempted as we are, yet without sin" (Heb. 4:15). Jesus already walked through every high and low you and I will ever encounter. However, He was never victimized by the circumstances that surrounded Him. Instead, He conquered.

Your Savior knows of every giant you'll face. He's not ignorant of what keeps you up at night. He knows you, and He knows what you grapple with. He knows the thoughts that bombard you day in and day out. More important still, He knows exactly what you need to hear to conquer your invisible enemies. He has provided the solution in His perfect sacrifice. He carried your issues on His back, all the way to the top of the hill where He was crucified. He made a way for you to be liberated from your struggles, fears, and insecurities once and for all.

There is no benefit in being problem-focused. Real transformation takes place when you see right through your problems (just as Joshua and Caleb did). Beyond the facade of every giant lies a solution: Christ Himself.

"You shall know the truth, and the truth shall make you free."
–John 8:32

As a Man Thinks in His Heart

Your mindsets and beliefs are a representation of your internal world, and they will always influence your external world. As the saying goes, "What you *think* about *comes* about." What you believe and hold in your heart and mind determines the world you experience. We are to bring all our thoughts and perspectives into alignment with what God says. This is renewing our minds with truth. We cannot allow ourselves to entertain thoughts outside of the reality of Christ's love and victory.

"For as he thinks in his heart, so is he."
– Proverbs 23:7

When you realize that the strongholds of fear, pride, and condemnation are in a constant battle to win your agreement, you must actively set your mind above, in the realm of Christ's victory.

Is Christ afraid? Is He condemned? Is He lost in pride? No! Then why should Christians entertain these voices for even a second? The more you behold the Solution, the less you will find yourself ensnared by these three earthly, sensual, and demonic strongholds.

"For the weapons of our warfare are not carnal but mighty in God for pulling down strongholds, casting down arguments and every high thing that exalts itself against the knowledge of God, bringing every thought into captivity to the obedience of Christ..."
– 2 Corinthians 10:4-5

The true warfare of our day is not in trying to modify our behaviors to live free from fear, pride, or condemnation. The warfare we should be concerned with is the ongoing responsibility to take every thought captive. We must recognize that our thought life is too valuable to allow old lies to have free reign. The mind is our battleground, and the outcome is life or death.

Will you choose to partner with truth and experience the abundant life Jesus promised, or will you give in to these old mindsets that wreak havoc and produce destructive behaviors? This choice does not need to be difficult. We are loved, chosen, and empowered by God to succeed. God's grace is the divine ability to choose right thoughts, speech, and actions.

"One thing I do, forgetting those things which are behind and reaching forward to those things which are ahead, I press toward the goal for the prize of the upward call of God in Christ Jesus."
– Philippians 3:13-14

Let go of the past. Let go of your performance. Let go of everything that's defined who you say you are. Leave it where it belongs: behind you! Grace empowers you to see the victory that's already yours.

Many Christians are still hard-wired according to a common way of thinking: the law. However, the life-changing truth of Jesus Christ is that you are *already* righteous. Let's take a deeper look at this topic.

Chapter Two

The Law and Grace

When it comes to conquering your giants, there are no formulas. No laws, rules, or regulations could ever empower you to reign in life. The law only strengthens the sins, lies, and issues you fight to overcome (see 1 Cor. 15:56). You can never out-perform your giants. However, Jesus can, and He already did! When you realize the power of Christ in you, the adversary will cower in fear. The first step to freedom is leaving Egypt behind by forsaking the law of sin and death.

I have noticed that when the people I disciple do not find their identity in Christ, they reduce themselves to nothing more than "sinners" in their own minds. Because of their beliefs, they are stuck in repeating cycles of failure. In their minds, they are trapped in a cage of their past mistakes, the environments they grew up in, and their families' dysfunctional histories. They are continually saying to themselves, *I want to do right, but I find myself always doing the opposite of what I want to do* (see Rom. 7:15-20). There seems to be no way out of the constant war against sin. They find themselves defeated and hopeless. Their physical energy levels decrease, and they become burned out and seemingly useless for the call of God on their lives.

You may find yourself in this place, thinking those same thoughts: *Is there any rest for me? Who can save me from this cycle of sin I'm in?* Jesus already has! You no longer have to be beaten, battered, and bruised in the battle against sin. Jesus already was! So what is trapping you in this cycle? The only thing keeping you in this war for your Promised Land is *you*. You have the choice to trust His victory or to trust in your own performance.

What Does the Law Look Like?

In some Christian circles, "the law" is highly praised, with an intense focus given to the Ten Commandments of Moses. In other grace-centered cultures, it is avoided like the plague. My desire is to show what the Law was, how it operated under the Old Covenant, and how people still live under it today.

When I refer to living under "the law," I am not only referencing the Ten Commandments or the levitical rules and regulations given in the Old Testament. I am referring to an entire way of thinking.

To put it simply, the law says, "You *are* what you *do*."

If you steal, you're a thief. If you drink too much, you're a drunk. If you struggle with pornography, you're an porn-addict. The law assigns identity based on your mistakes and then leaves you to your own devices. In order to be loved, you must act in a loveable way. In order to be righteous, you have to do a bunch of righteous deeds. In order to be holy, you have to fast, pray, and read your Bible. You perform for love, fight for righteousness, and hide when you realize you can't measure up.

Under the law, we sign an agreement with punishment. We agree to get what we deserve. However, when we accepted Christ, we also agreed to get what *He* deserves. So, what would you rather have? The punishment you deserve, or the blessing He deserves?

If we believe "we are what we do," we receive the consequence of that belief. We enter into a fight with the sin we believe we struggle with. We find that we have no grace to overcome and are stuck in patterns of constant failure. However, when we believe our righteousness comes from the actions of Jesus and our justification by His sacrifice, we can receive righteousness by God's grace.

It's vital that we identify ourselves according to what we see in Scripture. "Therefore, if anyone is in Christ, he is a new creation; old things have passed away; behold, all things have become new" (2 Cor. 5:17). If you accept the truth and believe you are new, rivers of living water will flow from within you (see John 7:38). Allow your heart to treasure His words beyond what you see, think, or feel, and you will see your victory come to pass. "Keep your heart with all diligence, for out of it spring the issues of life" (Prov. 4:23).

Justified Apart from the Law

"Therefore the law was our tutor to bring us to Christ, that we might be justified by faith."
– Galatians 3:24

The law itself is not the issue. In fact, Paul writes that the law is perfect, holy, spiritual, and just (Rom. 7:12). The law was given for the purpose of tutoring us. It teaches us the dangers of sin. If it were not for the law, we would not know what sin is.

The problem of the law is not with the law itself but with using the law to earn righteousness.

The law was not meant to perfect us but to open our eyes to our imperfection. The law holds such a high standard of holiness that we find we are incapable of measuring up. This points us to the need for justification apart from our actions. Relying on our own ability to do right subjects us to the consequences of the law when we fail.

We have the choice to work for ourselves or let God's work shine through us. For example, if I choose to fight, flail, and panic when a lifeguard is trying to keep me from drowning, who am I depending on? Myself. But if I let go, relax, and remain patient, the lifeguard can do his or her job of rescuing me.

Jesus said, "Do not think that I have come to abolish the Law or the Prophets; I have not come to abolish them but to fulfill them" (Matt. 5:17). Jesus knew that the law had no flaw. It was man that was flawed and unable to live perfectly by its many rules. However, Jesus lived a holy life as a man under the law, completely fulfilling it. When He died on the Cross, He took our failure upon Himself, even though He was spotless. Through this exchange, we are made righteous. "For our sake He made Him to be sin who knew no sin, so that in Him we might become the righteousness of God" (2 Cor. 5:21). Jesus fulfilled the requirements of the law on our behalf so that we could be made perfect apart from it.

"For by one offering He has perfected
for all time those who are sanctified."
– Hebrews 10:14

Are You Perfect?

There are two different roads we can take in an attempt to be made perfect. The first is self-effort. On this road, we try to live a perfect life through hard work. This is exactly what Adam and Eve did. They tried to become like God through their actions. Taking this road activates the system of the law in our lives, ensuring we get what we deserve. However, the righteous don't live by works but by faith (see Rom. 1:17).

This brings us to the second road to perfection: the free gift. On this road, we understand that righteousness comes as the result of humble, yielded faith. We can only live righteously when we first realize that, in and of ourselves, we do not have the ability. We need something—or Someone—to give righteousness as a gift; a gift that will empower us to walk in holiness, purity, and conviction.

When I preach on righteousness, I will often use the following illustration. I ask, "Raise your hand if you believe you are perfect." Normally, two or three people raise their hands, and the majority of the room looks around, confused.

Next, I will ask, "Now, raise your hand if you believe you are perfect in Christ." Almost the whole room will raise their hand.

Immediately following, I say, "Raise your hand if you are in Christ." Everyone raises their hand for this one.

Then I do it again. "Now, raise your hand if you are perfect." People hesitantly raise their hands.

I will repeat this one or two more times until everyone keeps their hands raised. By then, the congregation has caught on, and they start to see what I am hinting at. When people do not believe they are perfect, it reveals that they are not seeing themselves in Christ. They have separated their identity from Christ's and are still holding themselves in judgment according to the law. People sometimes get offended at this because they still look at their own works to define themselves rather than the finished work of Christ. If you are in Christ, you are perfect just as He is perfect!

"Love has been perfected among us in this:
that we may have boldness in the day of judgment;
because as He is, so are we in this world."
– 1 John 4:17

But if I'm perfect, why do I continue doing the things I don't want to do and cannot seem to do the things I want to do (see Rom. 7:15-20)? It is because we have law-based thinking and are focused on ourselves and our actions. Since the fall of man, humanity has been self-focused and conditioned according to the law. We were brought under a system of self-righteousness that relies on our own efforts to defend, justify, and protect ourselves.

This way of thinking is deceptive. The person who attempts to live rightly without depending on Jesus will never get out of sin. You cannot do it on your own because you were never designed to. We are helpless to protect ourselves from sin. We are incapable of justifying ourselves. How can we who are dirty make ourselves clean? It's impossible to get clean by bathing in dirty water. You have to be cleansed with pure water. Likewise, we need the pure water of His righteousness to cleanse us from the filthy rags of our own righteousness. Come to Him and let Him wash you clean! Stop trying to reach holiness alone.

He's Prepared a Table

Stop trying to better yourself by your own works. Stop trying to bite your lip and white-knuckle your way out of sin. Stop offering sacrifices of your own works to earn favor with God. Stop trying to earn His affection for you. Stop thinking you are what you do. Stop judging your heart's intentions behind every action.

It's time to start reigning in life. Remember, "those who receive abundance of grace and of the gift of righteousness will reign in life through the One, Jesus Christ" (Rom. 5:17). The key is to receive. We think to ourselves, *It can't be that easy... you don't understand. I've tried everything to get rid of this issue in my life*. But it really is that simple with Christ! The system of self-righteousness has left us believing that we have to do all the warring against sin and the enemy. However, God has provided a solution to give us righteousness freely, apart from striving. If we allow Christ to be the fulfillment of the law and the propitiation for our sins, we will walk in the true freedom Christ bought for us.

"You prepare a table before me in the presence of my enemies; You anoint my head with oil; my cup overflows. Surely Your goodness and love will follow me all the days of my life, and I will dwell in the house of the Lord forever."
– Psalm 23:5-6 NIV

According to God, battling against our enemies looks like sitting down to feast at the table He has prepared for us. You only eat in front of your enemies when you are confident they are not a threat and when you believe you are already victorious. Those with a "law" mindset try to figure out what they need to do in order to fight and become victorious. He has prepared a table in front of our enemies, yet we still try to figure out what we need to bring to dinner. All He asks is that we take a seat! All God wants you to do is partake of Jesus, choose truth, and accept His free gift of righteousness.

What Does Grace Look Like?

"I will give you a new heart and put a new spirit within you; I will take the heart of stone out of your flesh and give you a heart of flesh."
– Ezekiel 36:26

When Jesus hung on the Cross, He spoke these famous words: "It is finished." The question is, "*What* is finished?"

Jesus fulfilled the law. There's not a single law left to be accomplished or performed. Jesus came to put the old system of "right and wrong" to an end. "For Christ is the end of the law for righteousness to everyone who believes" (Rom. 10:4).

Never again will you need to modify your actions to be considered righteous in God's sight. God has moved away from the temple system of sacrifices and burnt offerings. Now, He is looking at your heart. He is transcribing His very personality, character, and attributes onto the blood-washed canvas of your inner man. The law is no longer your tutor. The Spirit of Christ has been hardwired into your DNA. You are a new creation. When Christ said, "It is finished," He meant it!

"And by Him everyone who believes is justified from all things from which you could not be justified by the law of Moses."
– Acts 13:39

Many confuse grace and mercy. While mercy forgives us for what we've done and allows us to live free from the consequences of sin, grace empowers us to live completely free from sin. Grace is the empowerment of Christ to live in righteousness. It is not a cover-up for evil. It is the supernatural power to overcome it. Grace abolishes sin and establishes a new nature. Grace is the key to the transformed Christian life. It alone will conform us to the image of Christ.

When we stop striving to earn favor with God, we open ourselves up to receive His grace apart from our actions. By surrendering to the Gospel and accepting the free gift of righteousness, we become targets for the empowering presence of God. An exchange has taken place: our strength for His.

Taking it further, when we "awaken to righteousness," we "sin not" (see 1 Cor. 15:34). We let go of the law when we look at ourselves through the righteous blood of Christ. We find that we are supernaturally able to overcome the things we struggled with before. Cycles are broken, bad habits lose their edge, and freedom begins to grow from within.

Proverbs 23:7 says, "For as he thinks in his heart, so is he." *Well, I sure do think a lot of bad things. Does that mean I'm wicked?* No. The good news is that Christ took care of our heart issue. We've been given *new* hearts and *new* minds in Christ. He has taken out the hearts of stone and replaced them with hearts of flesh. This new heart guarantees that we are righteous and holy by nature. We have been united with the Spirit of Holiness Himself! That is the power of grace!

"Since, then, we do not have the excuse of ignorance, everything—and I do mean everything—connected with that old way of life has to go. It's rotten through and through. Get rid of it! And then take on an entirely new way of life— a God-fashioned life, a life renewed from the inside and working itself into your conduct as God accurately reproduces his character in you."
– Ephesians 4:20-24 (MSG)

So, here you stand; the old system of the law has passed. Your conscience has been washed clean, you have been set free from the cycle of dead works, and now God is doing a new thing. Even as you're reading this book, He is taking you further than you've ever gone before. As we take on these giants of fear, pride, and condemnation, remember it's not up to your effort or performance—it's all about Him. His love, humility, and righteousness will transform us into His image. The solution is always Jesus!

Chapter Three

Fear and Love

Fear is a tenacious enemy against God's power in our lives. It's a dog with all bark and no bite. Fear masquerades itself as "logical" and "safe," but it completely contradicts our purposes in Christ. It wants more than anything for you to feel like a grasshopper in your own sight. However, the truth is that every giant we face in Christ is like a splattered bug on the windshield of our lives—powerless.

For a clearer definition of what fear is, let's look at the Word: "There is no fear in love; but perfect love casts out fear, because fear involves torment. But he who fears has not been made perfect in love" (1 John 4:18). John clearly draws the line between fear and love. Fear opposes God because God *is* love.

Paul echoes John's assessment in 2 Timothy 1:7: "For God has not given us a spirit of fear, but of power and of love and of a sound mind." Simply put, fear isn't in God's vocabulary, so it shouldn't be in ours.

Fear of the Lord vs. the Spirit of Fear

I want to make a quick distinction between the fear of the Lord and the spirit of fear. The former is a separate concept discussed throughout Scripture and is quite different from the spirit of fear. Proverbs 14:27 says, "The fear of the Lord is a fountain of life, that one may avoid the snares of death." This is a far cry from the "torment" of the spirit of fear discussed in 1 John. King David also had much to say about the fear of the Lord:

"Oh, how great is Your goodness, which You have laid up for those who fear You, which You have prepared for those who trust in you in the presence of the sons of men!"
– Psalm 31:19

David was convinced that God has good things prepared for those who fear Him. Fearing the Lord can be characterized as a reverent decision to trust, surrender, and love Him above all else. It is a simple yet powerful acknowledgment of God as God and a choice to serve none other.

The fear of the Lord is awe, honor, and respect toward God in a posture of humility. A person who fears the Lord understands that He is the Almighty Creator, the Potter who formed the clay (see Is. 64:8). This understanding invites the favor of God.

"But on this one will I look:
on him who is poor and of a contrite spirit,
and who trembles at My word."
– Isaiah 66:2

Now, this doesn't mean you're afraid of being punished by Him. The Hebrew word translated as "fear" in these passages implies a strong reverence for the Lord. Someone who fears the Lord honors His Word. Throughout Scripture, we see people tremble when they hear God speak to them. His voice creates an immediate and noticeable shift that causes even the earth to shake (see Heb. 12:26). Just as the sound of His voice causes a dramatic shift in the earth, it can transform our patterns, cycles, and mindsets.

People wonder why they are unsatisfied, stressed, sleepless, and discouraged. Being fearful of punishment produces these symptoms, whereas the fear of the Lord leads to life and satisfaction. Think about it: He is the Creator of heaven and earth. He is omnipotent and mighty! He is the unstoppable God who has chosen to betroth you and make you His own. If He is for you, what could possibly stand against you?

How Does Fear Manifest?

The Gospel has forever bound fear by its wrists and ankles and washed it away in the ocean of God's unconditional love. Yet, despite the finished work, many Christians still struggle with fear every day in a variety of ways. This isn't because God hasn't already won. It's because they've yet to taste and see His goodness in its totality. There are many areas in our lives that are still waiting to experience the radical love of a good Father. Once we taste how truly merciful and kind He is, we can never be the same. The more we allow His love to saturate our hearts, the more we will radiate with His fearless nature.

Nowadays, many fears are written off as mental or psychological disorders: anxiety, panic attacks, and others. But fear is fear, and the solution remains the same: *love*. Jesus was well aware of anxiety, stress, and worry, and He spoke openly about it:

"Therefore I say to you, do not worry about your life, what you will eat or what you will drink; nor about your body, what you will put on...Which of you by worrying can add one cubit to his stature?...Therefore do not worry, saying, 'What shall we eat?' or 'What shall we drink?' or 'What shall we wear?'...For your heavenly Father knows that you need all these things. But seek first the kingdom of God and His righteousness, and all these things shall be added to you. Therefore do not worry about tomorrow, for tomorrow will worry about its own things..."

– Matthew 6:25, 27, 31-34 (emphasis added)

This is obviously not just a modern problem. Worry has been around since the fall of man. Stress, anxiety, panic attacks, and doubt can all be traced back to the root of fear. Corrie Ten Boom (a woman who helped Jewish people escape the Nazi regime during the Holocaust) said, "Worry is a cycle of inefficient thoughts, whirling around a center of fear." So how do we break this cycle? We remind ourselves that our Heavenly Father knows exactly what we need. He won't leave you stranded. He loves you, and He will supply your needs as you seek first His plans for your life.

Identifying Fear

Fear manifests in so many different ways that it might seem impossible to pin it down. Fortunately, identifying fear is often much easier than listing all of its variations. Here are a few indicators of fear that I have found very useful:

- Any area of your life where you are expecting judgment is an area where fear is at work. This is frequently how the law is misapplied. People wait for the punishment they think they deserve for their failures, often unknowingly living in fear through the process.
- Fear will always sound intimidating, attempting to make you believe it is more powerful than Christ within you. Fear is like a shadow that will turn into a monster if you believe in it. This is why the demonic often latches onto fear. It's not real, but it will try to make you believe it is.
- Another way to recognize fear is that it opposes thankfulness. It is self-focused and mirrors the direct opposite of 1 Corinthians 13's teaching on "love." (Remember what 1 John 4:18 has to say about how fear is the enemy of love.) The Bible directly addresses removing fear from your speech and choosing to be thankful.

"Be anxious for nothing, but in everything by prayer and supplication, with thanksgiving, let your requests be made known to God..."
– Philippians 4:6

- Fear attacks your identity. It will try to make you feel small, unqualified, and indecisive. If left unchecked, your identity will become a mere shell of what God meant for it to be.

- Look for how fear affects your life and the people around you. Perhaps it manifests as a constant state of anxiety, stress, or being overwhelmed. These indicators are often quite easy to see, as even Solomon revealed:

"Anxiety in the heart of man causes depression,
but a good word makes it glad."
– Proverbs 12:25

- Another major indicator of fear can be found in how you treat your leaders. How you view leaders is likely a reflection of how you view God in your life. If you fear them or only come to them when you make mistakes, you will often treat God the same way. This reveals a fear of punishment, vulnerability, and intimacy.

Three Access Points of Fear

It's important that we understand how fear enters our lives so we can stop it in its tracks. What opens the gate for fear to wreak havoc on our minds and lifestyles? The three main access points are our past, the law, and the lies we believe about our identity.

Many of us are conditioned from a young age to think with fearful mindsets. These come through the teaching of our parents and leaders and through traumatic experiences. The world and the people around us cement these mindsets in place, giving us a lack of trust in God's goodness and love. Even though your past may remind you of the reason you should be afraid and defensive, it should not be held above the Word of God. God has something quite different to say about fear:

"Fear not, for I am with you; be not dismayed,
for I am your God. I will strengthen you, Yes, I will help you,
I will uphold you with My righteous right hand."
– Isaiah 41:10

The law opens the door to fear. It misrepresents God's attitude toward who we are in the New Covenant. The law, justly, tells us that God is angry at us—He has punishment stored up for sin. It tells us that God's anger is inescapable and that we should expect Old Testament-like judgments. However, praise be to God; that is not our portion anymore!

"For when we were still without strength, in due time Christ died for the ungodly...But God demonstrates His own love toward us, in that while we were still sinners, Christ died for us. Much more then, having now been justified by His blood, we shall be saved from wrath through Him."
– Romans 5:6, 8-9

Believing we are still our old, sinful selves is another path through which fear enters. Forgetting our true identity will send us spiraling into fear because, as the Bible clearly says, there are many reasons to be afraid without God. The truth is, however, if we have surrendered our lives to Jesus Christ, God calls us His own beloved children (see 1 John 3:1). We now have no reason to be lost in fear anymore. Even the prophets in the Old Testament understood this:

"Fear not, for I have redeemed you; I have called you by your name; you are Mine."
– Isaiah 43:1

This is the Gospel! We should no longer fear because we have been claimed by another. We are no longer subject to our old identity: a lost, scared child of the world. We are now, as Isaiah 43:1 says, a people who have been "called by name." This is why we can fear not.

Fear in the Bible

Peter himself was confronted with crippling fear. Yes, even the "Rock upon which the church was built" (Matt. 16:18) fell under fear's powerful influence. In Matthew 26, we see his story:

"Now Peter sat outside in the courtyard. And a servant girl came to him, saying, 'You also were with Jesus of Galilee.' But he denied it before them all, saying, 'I do not know what you are saying.' And when he had gone out to the gateway, another girl saw him and said to those who were there, 'This fellow also was with Jesus of Nazareth.' But again he denied with an oath, 'I do not know the Man!' And a little later those who stood by came up and said to Peter, 'Surely you also are one of them, for your speech betrays you.' Then he began to curse and swear, saying, 'I do not know the Man!' Immediately a rooster crowed. And Peter remembered the word of Jesus who had said to him, 'Before the rooster crows, you will deny Me three times.' So he went out and wept bitterly."
– Matthew 26:69-75

Unfortunately for Peter, what may have been his biggest failure was birthed out of the fear of man. Peter's fear of people and what they might do to him caused him to renounce the Christ he had left everything to follow! Fear disillusioned him, and he hid. He wouldn't identify himself with Christ for fear of what would happen to him. He took on the characteristics of a victim and acted as if he were an entirely different person. Where was the Peter of a few chapters earlier who said he would never leave Christ? He had fallen under the toxic influence of fear.

Kicking Fear in the Face

I have personally seen fear impact and influence people countless times over the years. Quite often, I will stretch those I lead by challenging them to step outside their comfort zone in creative ways. My goal is never to create more fear by exposing or humiliating them. It is always to show them that they can conquer their fear, sometimes even by failing or looking foolish. Such situations will cause you to realize that your failure or embarrassment has no hold on you and cannot limit you. It breaks the power of fear!

I remember one time in particular when I asked a young man I was mentoring to sing in front of a group of people. He was nervous. In fact, he was petrified. He had never been comfortable singing in front of people before. The environment was safe, encouraging, and full of people who would love him regardless of his performance (which is important to consider when stretching someone you lead), but he was still terrified.

Despite the swirling fear, he opened his mouth and let his voice be heard. He completed the song with a shaky voice and sang off-key, but the group in front of him roared in applause. The event showed him that his fear of failing and "looking bad" in front of people was irrational. From then on, he was fearless to fail in that way because he had faced it before and had seen that his fear was powerless.

You will find victory when you stretch yourself to find peace within rather than allowing the fear of your external circumstances to dominate you. Once you center on Christ, every fear will bow to His peace and glorious power, freeing you to do many things (such as "making a fool" of yourself in front of others) without any reservation!

"These things I have spoken to you, that in Me you may have peace. In the world you will have tribulation; but be of good cheer, I have overcome the world."
—John 16:33

Jesus clearly believed that the peace within His followers would trump any fear or instability the world could throw at them. If you look at the context of the above verse, He was talking about fear scattering His disciples! He was telling them that, even though Peter would deny Him and others would flee in hopeless terror, His peace would still be more powerful.

The truth is that fear never has the final say. Jesus reversed the fall of man. Peter became one of the boldest preachers of the Gospel in recorded history. Likewise, that young man I mentored has now sung in front of hundreds of people with true peace and joy within him.

Fear vs. Faith Expressed Through Love

When you take time to critically examine fear, you see that it is simply the expectation of punishment or pain. Fear sees the worst possible outcome. *Do not speak up; you will just say something wrong! Be careful not to stand out; people will laugh at you! Do not confess that sin; you will be judged. Hide your mistake so that you will not get punished!* All of these thoughts are fear-driven. Those who fear expect the pain of a negative consequence more than the joy of the Holy Spirit supporting and strengthening them.

As I have mentioned, 1 John 4:18 explains that "he who fears has not been made perfect in love." He who fears expects punishment or a negative outcome from a situation. The key to overcoming fear is simple. You must understand that you are truly, deeply loved by God—and that's not just a spiritual declaration quoted by Christians! It is a reality with tangible benefits and blessings that surround your life.

When you love someone, you will do anything for them. If danger was coming their way, you would do everything in your power to stop it. It is the same with God. In fact, He is far better than our human understanding of love. His definition of love is selfless and sacrificial. His love casts out fear because it instills confidence in us that is stronger than any fear.

At its core, fear is False Evidence Appearing Real. It has more trust in the enemy's lies and accusations than in God's promises and protection. The only way to grow more confident in these attributes of God is to grow in relationship with Him. When you know who He is by experiencing Him, you will never doubt His nature.

Walking the Tightrope

Have you ever heard of the legendary tightrope walker Charles Blondin? He gained his fame by being the first person to cross Niagara Falls on a tightrope in the summer of 1859. He crossed the misty gorge, spanning over 1,000 feet, at least eight times that summer. Blondin's notoriety spread, and the crowds grew on each occasion. Everyone wanted to see this daredevil make the crossing from Canada to America on a rope only 3 inches thick! As if that were not a feat in itself, Blondin performed a variety of stunts along the way, including somersaulting, backflipping, pushing a wheelbarrow, walking on stilts, and standing on a balanced chair!

One of the most remarkable performances occurred on August 14th when Blondin carried his manager, Harry Colcord, across the Niagara Gorge. Before they crossed, Blondin shared this advice to Colcord: "Look up, Harry...you are no longer Colcord; you are Blondin...be a part of me, mind, body, and soul. If I sway, sway with me. Do not attempt to do any balancing yourself. If you do, we will both go to our death."

It is one thing to believe that Blondin could carry someone across, but it is an entirely different matter to be the one on Blondin's back. That is faith in action. I believe Colcord could climb on his friend's back because he knew Blondin was trustworthy. Notice the instruction Blondin gave: "Do not attempt to do any balancing yourself." Success would come when Colcord calmed his fears and trusted.

This story beautifully illustrates our walk with the Lord. We know who He is by experiencing Him, listening to His voice, and seeing Him in the Word. When we know His love for us, we have confidence in His ability to protect, save, deliver, heal, and turn any situation for good. In this place, it is very difficult for fear to take hold. God has a 100% success rate. There is no chance of Him falling, and, as His son or daughter, you are one with Him. When He sways, you sway with Him. And, best of all, you do not have to do any of the balancing! Your Heavenly Father is trustworthy, and there is no reason for fear.

"The steadfast love of the Lord never ceases; his mercies never come to an end; they are new every morning; great is your faithfulness."
– Lamentations 3:22-23 ESV

When Fear Comes Knocking

When fear comes knocking at your door, do not answer it! It has no right to your life and no right to attach itself to your identity. You are not a victim of fear. In that moment, you have the power to choose to believe the truth. You have the ability to shut fear down and partner with faith. Entertaining the lying voice of fear never leads to profitable thinking. It usually leads to more fear and can often usher in the voice of condemnation or pride as well.

Whatever we give our attention to will always influence us. Even worse, when we give our attention to something other than the promises and person of God, we worship it as an idol. God is the only one worthy of our focus and praise.

When you see that everything comes back to seeing, knowing, and being loved by Jesus, fear's voice is silenced. If you fixate on living a life that serves yourself, fear's voice can seem like a familiar friend. It whispers to you, advising you against living by the Spirit or trusting the promises of God.

Choose to embrace the treasure of your new life: freedom from the voice of fear. Remember that you have the choice. You now have the power to reject the lies of fear and embrace the promises of new life and relationship with God. We can cast our burdens on Him because He cares for us (see 1 Peter 5:7). He is our salvation. What do we need to fear?

"Take My yoke upon you and learn from Me, for I am gentle and lowly in heart, and you will find rest for your souls. For My yoke is easy and My burden is light."
– Matthew 11:29-30

I want to finish this chapter with a testimony from one of the leaders on my team. He was faced with anxiety, fear, and torment in his mind. Through a choice to believe in God's reality over his own feelings, all of it fell away!

Nathan's Story

During one of our monthly house meetings, Daniel, our house pastor, began asking us all how we were doing. Around this point in the night, I started getting hot and feeling pressure on my head, to the point that I even got up to get a glass of water. I had a feeling the pressure was demonic, but I was too scared to bring it up. I internally hoped Daniel would take notice and call it out so I wouldn't have to myself. Sure enough, sensing that something was off with me, Daniel began asking me questions to see how I was doing, to which I explained the pressure on my head, etc.

I remember that I was dealing with a lot that year. I had a great deal of anxiety and fear because I didn't have the money to pay the remainder of my tuition for school. I felt overwhelmed by my workload. I had been in an ongoing state of anxiety about the well-being of my parents, and I was still learning how to navigate the reality of their separation. My expectations for friendships and connection with the people I was running with that year were being let down, and I had so much fear of rejection and hurt. My dog died. My dad was depressed. And to top it off, I was falling back into an emotional spiral and addictions I thought I had left behind.

That night, Daniel fathered me. He challenged me to face the fear and cloudiness that had been tormenting me. He asked me to stand up and speak to the demonic with authority to leave, but I couldn't. He led me to imagine two bullies tormenting me (one of them was fear). He guided me to boldly stand up to them and tell them to go. I did, but I was too afraid and had no confidence in the words I was saying. Then, he asked me to declare the truth. I struggled with this too. The only scripture that came to my mind in that moment was Romans 8:38-39, and so I spoke out, "For I am persuaded that neither death nor life, nor angels nor principalities nor powers, nor things present nor things to come, nor height nor depth, nor any other created thing, shall be able to separate us from the love of God which is in Christ Jesus our Lord."

Next, he told me to sing. Anyone who knows me knows I love to sing out loud. But I was afraid that night to sing. It was like something was covering my mouth, and I just couldn't bring myself to do it. I even asked if I could pray loudly instead. Nope.

Daniel encouraged me and waited for me to find the courage to sing. Finally, with tears streaming down my face, I sang out the words, "Nothing could ever separate me from the love of Jesus. It's mine forever. I'm yours forever."

"Again," Daniel said. I sang it again. "Again," Daniel said. I continued to sing it softly at first but grew increasingly louder, more confident, more bold, and more authoritative each time. Before I knew it, I was practically shout-singing this in our living room, and then I felt a shift. The heaviness lifted, and I was left weeping, so aware of God's love for me. The room felt clearer and lighter. I opened my eyes, and my housemates, mentors, and Daniel were all looking at me. They all felt the shift too. We all proceeded to worship the Lord together in song.

That night, for one of the first times in my life, I came face to face with fear and realized the might and authority God has given me not to be a victim but to conquer it. He showed me the power that's in my voice to silence the lies of the enemy and that I have the capacity to rise above.

Fear is Finished

This is an amazing testimony! God's love cast out fear in Nathan, and He wants to do the same in you. When Jesus died for you, it wasn't a one-time act of love. His Cross is an everlasting statement that echoes into eternity. If He loved you enough to die for you, how do you think He feels about you now? It's easy to write off God's love as a history lesson found in an ancient book, but that isn't the case. "The Lord has appeared of old to me, saying: 'Yes, I have loved you with an everlasting love; therefore with lovingkindness I have drawn you'" (Jer. 31:3). The love we read about in the Bible is an everlasting love. Just as Nathan sang, nothing is separating you from the love of God in Christ Jesus.

Fear is forever finished because love has been forever established. When you behold the Cross, fear's voice becomes so small. The greatest act of love ever committed is shining forth, speaking to us today. His Cross extends beyond the barriers of time and reaches us in this present moment. Through it, the Lord is speaking, "I love you. Even after that mistake, I love you. Even when you feel inadequate, I love you. Don't be afraid. I love you. Look at the holes in My hands and My feet. I will never change My mind about you. My scars are an everlasting declaration of My vast affection for you. *I love you!*"

"He who did not spare His own Son, but delivered Him up for us all, how shall He not with Him also freely give us all things?"
—Romans 8:32

When you see His love displayed, the only logical response is to abandon fear and wholeheartedly trust Him.

Chapter Four

Pride and Humility

Pride sounds a lot like Goliath. It thinks it has everything figured out, yet it lives in a fantasy land, detached from the empowering presence of God. It pumps itself up, believing it is the biggest and greatest warrior in the land. For Goliath, this may have actually been the case. He was an incredibly strong and gifted soldier—but he wasn't connected to the God of Angel Armies. He was independent and rogue, selfish and boastful.

"And when the Philistine looked about and saw David, he disdained him; for he was only a youth, ruddy and good-looking. So the Philistine said to David, 'Am I a dog, that you come to me with sticks?' And the Philistine cursed David by his gods. And the Philistine said to David, 'Come to me, and I will give your flesh to the birds of the air and the beasts of the field'" (1 Sam. 17:42-44)! These would become his famous last words. Pride comes before the fall, and Goliath had a long way to fall.

This Goliath-like pride is built on confidence in yourself rather than in God. The entire fall of man can be traced back to pride, when Adam and Eve chose to eat from the Tree of the Knowledge of Good and Evil. They chose to pursue their own understanding of right and wrong over God's. They lacked nothing and had a perfect, unhindered relationship with the Lord. Then, they were deceived into stepping out of their God-given identity and attempted to create their own identity. Mankind was already created in God's image in the very beginning. The Lord spoke, "Let Us make man in Our image, according to Our likeness" (Gen. 1:26).

"Then the serpent said to the woman, 'You will not surely die. For God knows that in the day you eat of it your eyes will be opened, and you will be like God, knowing good and evil.'"
– Genesis 3:4-5

They were already like God! They did not trust what God had said about them and behaved from a place of pride, assuming they had found the solution to a problem they didn't even have. Their confidence was more in themselves than in what God had spoken. Their actions polluted humanity from that day forward with the sickness of self. In reality, pride is usually a mask that covers a lack of true confidence. Someone who knows his or her God-given identity may be confident but is far from prideful.

It is pride that turns the gift of life into a rat race of self-fulfillment. Those in pride believe they deserve certain blessings or benefits. The prideful person thinks to himself or herself: *I can do it by myself. I don't need help. My way is the best way. I am better than that person because I've accomplished this or behaved like that.*

C.S. Lewis writes, "As long as you are proud you cannot know God. A proud man is always looking down on things and people: and, of course, as long as you are looking down you cannot see something that is above you." When you see it plainly, a person in pride is operating selfishly. Selfishness is the behavior of pride, just as selflessness is the behavior of humility.

"God resists you when you are proud
but continually pours out grace when you are humble."
– James 4:6 TPT

God's opposition to pride is not a crusade against all prideful people or a smiting with thunderbolts. He hates pride because it builds a self-serving wall around you, blocking you from the flow of His grace. It leaves you to reap the consequences of your actions apart from God's favor and mercy. In this scenario, there is no grace to empower you because you falsely proclaim that you don't need anyone else. On the other hand, humility opens you to receive God's ability and divine favor. Feeling entitled to the Lord's benefits and blessings by your own actions keeps you far from receiving them. God doesn't owe you anything. He has already paid for everything, and you can't earn what has already been purchased.

Pride Comes Before the Fall

In Daniel 4, we see a ruler, King Nebuchadnezzar, brought low by pride. One evening, as he surveyed his kingdom on the rooftop of his palace, he said, "Is this not Babylon the great, which *I myself* have built as a royal residence by the might of *my* power and for the glory of *my* majesty?" (Dan. 4:30 NIV, emphasis added). In that moment, a voice from heaven spoke, "King Nebuchadnezzar, to you it is declared: sovereignty has been removed from you, and you will be driven away from mankind...until you recognize that the Most High is ruler over the realm of mankind and bestows it on whomever He wishes" (Dan. 4:32 NASB 1995). When Nebuchadnezzar claimed responsibility for what only God could do, the Lord humbled him. God caused him to lose his mind for seven whole years, living among the beasts of the field and eating grass. At the end of that time, the king realized the greatness and sovereignty of God and gave honor and glory to Whom it was due.

This story illustrates the principle outlined in Proverbs 16:18: "Everyone who is proud in heart is an abomination to the Lord...Pride goes before destruction, and a haughty spirit before a fall." God hates pride. The intensity of this hatred is seen in the root word of pride: *ga'own*. This Hebrew word means "exaltation, majesty, pride." Used in the context of God, it is translated as "majesty, splendor, or excellence." The same word, used in the context of mankind, is almost always translated as "pride." This implies that *ga'own,* in a positive sense, is something that describes God and belongs to God alone, not man.

"The wicked in his proud countenance does not seek God;
God is in none of his thoughts."
– Psalm 10:4

When God is not in the picture, you are almost always in pride. What right does the clay have to determine its purpose without the Potter? Who are we, the creation, to say that we have no need for our Creator? When God is not an instrumental part of our day-to-day lives, we are either far too comfortable or far too dependent on ourselves. When Jesus teaches the core foundations of a fruitful life to His disciples in John 15, He says, "apart from Me you can do nothing." There is nothing fruitful we can produce on this earth apart from God. He is the source. He is life. He is everything.

"For by Him all things were created that are in heaven and that are on earth, visible and invisible, whether thrones or dominions or principalities or powers. All things were created through Him and for Him. And He is before all things, and in Him all things consist."
– Colossians 1:16-17

The children of Israel, in their journey to the Promised Land, stepped into prideful thinking when they forgot the miraculous provision and deliverance of God. They did not pass down the testimonies of God's works. They became more focused on their circumstances, which produced complaining, instead of remaining thankful and trusting in God's faithfulness. They even longed to return to slavery which was a complete insult to God's plan for their nation.

Pride comes when we detach ourselves from God and embrace unthankfulness and self-centeredness. Because of the way our feelings, emotions, and worldly principles have tutored us, we are prone to trust our own wisdom and ways more than God's. Whenever we trust ourselves more than God, we are building our foundations on sand!

Think about Jesus' parable of the two builders in Matthew 7. Both men heard the Word. They received God's instruction, but one man valued it above his own understanding and put it into practice. The other man did not. The storms of life came to both, but the difference between the two structures was whether they were built on sand or stone. We must build our lives on the solid foundation of God's Word rather than our own understanding and efforts. Take serious care to keep God's Word above your own understanding. If not, you are operating in pride.

Letting Go of Independence

A distinctive way pride manifests is in our interactions with leadership and earthly authority. It is one thing for a person to boast, "I trust God completely." However, it is an entirely different matter to trust God to the point that you trust those He has placed above you, whether bosses, pastors, mentors, or parents. After all, "the steps of a good man are ordered by the Lord" (Psalm 37:23), so we can trust that the leaders we have are those God has led us to serve. "There is no authority except from God, and the authorities that exist are appointed by God" (Rom. 13:1). True humility honors and submits to leaders.

Do you trust God's direction? Do you see that He has intentionally placed authority in your life? If you do, then part of trust and humility looks like trusting the counsel and guidance of another more than yourself. (This, of course, is built upon the premise that your leader is established in the Word and led by God's Spirit in his or her daily decisions.)

A quick test is to ask yourself, "Do I have someone in my life that I trust more than myself?" If the answer is no, I would strongly encourage you to find a leader, someone whom you respect, who is willing to speak into your life. This is a practical way to begin to trust the opinion of others above your own understanding. For more on this topic, check out my book *The Lost Art of Discipleship.*

The root of pride is relying on our own understanding. This directly opposes the Word of God in Proverbs 3:5-6: "Trust in the Lord with all your heart, and lean *not on your own understanding*; In all your ways acknowledge Him, and He shall direct your paths" (emphasis added). Trust looks like allowing God and those He has established as leaders in our lives to give us input. It is very likely, if not certain, that they have a broader perspective than we do and are only working for our best interests. Humbly trusting God and the leaders He has placed in your life is a freeing act! Not only does it release you from pridefully forcing your way to the top, but it embraces a tender relationship of intimacy and dependence on God.

The beauty of our Christian walk is that we are no longer responsible for directing our paths, determining right and wrong, or possessing the knowledge of good and evil. God invites us to lay aside our labors, performance, and even our need to understand. These are all old, independent mindsets seeking self-significance. In their place, we can receive the yoke of Christ, which is easy and light. This yoke brings rest to the weary soul tired of fighting for itself.

"The wise of this world in their pride often miss the treasures which the simple-hearted find on their knees," wrote A.W. Tozer. I wonder how many people live religiously, attempting to stand right before God or their peers, but are dying on the inside. Sadly, they will never attain the satisfaction they crave. A great tragedy is that so many believers overlook the treasure of grace that is available to all who humble themselves and receive it by faith.

The Mask of Pride

You can almost always find the fear of condemnation hiding behind the mask of pride. Think of the classic high school bully who mistreats his peers because, deep down, he feels insecure, lonely, or mistreated. He is behaving that way to feel powerful because on the inside he feels powerless, weak, and insignificant. Here, we see a place where the three roots are intertwined. The bully knows there is something wrong with him (condemnation). So instead of being exposed (fear), he acts out with aggressive and self-important tendencies (pride). The fear of punishment is a product of condemnation, and it fuels the choice to put on a mask of pride.

Many times, I have seen someone fall into sin, such as looking at pornography, lying, or stealing. Because they feel ashamed and fear punishment, they hide. Although this is motivated by fear, hiding is really a behavior of pride because it says, "I know the 'better' thing to do in this situation. I can fix myself. I can clean up my own mess. I don't need help." It is the same as Adam and Eve hiding behind fig leaves in the Garden of Eden. A person will rely on his or her own actions to hide their sin, leading to denial and a defiled conscience. They rely on their ability to improve (or cover) themselves instead of humbly letting God forgive and restore them.

Pride is fully conscious of sin but chooses to deny it or hide it with self-righteousness. Fig leaves are far inferior to the perfect sacrifice God offers to those who will receive it in humility. That is why God "gives grace to the humble" (Prov. 3:34). Grace is the transformational power that enables us to step into our new creation identity. Until you can honestly acknowledge your dependence on God, you will never receive the grace to live as a new man or woman.

Pride is not your natural identity. It is not an attractive mask. Francis Frangipane explains the danger of pride, warning us that "God can never entrust His Kingdom to anyone who has not been broken of pride, for pride is the armor of darkness itself."

Pride will cause you to pretend to be better than you are. It will identify *you* as the protector, leader, and source of your life instead of God. The voice of pride leads people to hide imperfections and shortcomings. *If anyone sees your weakness, you will be exposed for who you are: a weak, dirty sinner. If they saw your sin, you would be condemned.* Do you see how this is all connected? Pride manifests as a result of condemnation, usually motivated by fear.

The only reason anyone is afraid to remove his or her mask of pride is that it might jeopardize his or her self-image. The problem with that line of thinking is that it puts the responsibility back onto self, which is the very thing Jesus died to set you free from. We are called to lay down our lives, pick up our cross, and follow Jesus, who set the perfect example of humility.

Embracing Humility

"Let this mind be in you which was also in Christ Jesus, who, being in the form of God, did not consider it robbery to be equal with God, but made Himself of no reputation, taking the form of a bondservant, and coming in the likeness of men. And being found in appearance as a man, He humbled Himself and became obedient to the point of death, even the death of the cross."
– Philippians 2:5-8

Humility is the key. I cannot emphasize this enough. Humility comes when we are grounded in the character of Christ. We are the disciples of Jesus, called to imitate Him. Jesus chose to humble Himself, become a bondservant to us, and make Himself obedient to the point of death (see Phil. 2:5-8). Similarly, we must humble ourselves by recognizing that we cannot save ourselves. We must leave our selfish-ambitions behind, and follow Jesus—no matter where He leads us. When we lay our lives down on the altar of His Lordship, true life springs forth. As illogical as it sounds, when you die, you live. Humility undertstands that without God you are a dead man walking.

It is a beautiful thing to come to the end of yourself because that is the very place God begins. "My grace is sufficient for you, for My strength is made perfect in weakness" (2 Cor. 12:9). If only we knew that the moment we let go of our old life, we would receive the grace to live out a new one. Our new identity *is* humble because Christ lives in us, and He is the embodiment of humility. The more we spend time with Him, the more His influence will increase in our lives. We need to set time apart to be in His presence, in prayer, and in worship. As you see Him for who He is, you start to see who you really are, and there, transformation takes place.

If you see pride as a hindrance in your life, do not strive to appear humble. That sounds counterintuitive, but it is key. You are not the one responsible to fix your own problems. You are responsible to receive His grace by placing your faith in His ability to finish the work He has started in you. You are not responsible to be aware of problems but to maintain awareness of the problem-solver and His truth. Set yourself before Christ and look into His eyes. Let His love melt away the mask. He is not afraid of your sins or imperfections, and He is not condemning you. He has no punishment to give. He gives new life, radiant light, and unending love!

The Forgotten Core Value

Many of us hear prophetic words and the exciting promises God has for each of us and become instantly infatuated with our own destiny. It is not wrong to believe in a bright future with God. In fact, everyone who was around Jesus began to dream and come alive with hope. The problem comes when we allow our rational minds to dictate the *timeline* of the fulfilled promises.

You might recall the infamous story from Genesis 15 when God gave His promise to Abram (later Abraham) that his descendants would outnumber the stars in the night sky. However, his wife, Sarai (later Sarah), suggested that he sleep with her handmaiden, Hagar, because of her own old age and barrenness. When Hagar conceived and bore her son Ishmael, God restated His promise and assured Abram that Sarai would indeed bear a child. It was through this child, Isaac, that the nation of Israel would come and, eventually, the promised Messiah.

You see, trying to fulfill a promise in your own strength is like creating an "Ishmael." It is the prideful reliance on your own ability instead of trusting God's ability. Let us live with Abraham's renewed perspective, "being fully convinced that what [God] had promised He [is] also able to perform" (Rom. 4:21). When you have yet to see the "Isaac," do not try to control the situation through your own pride. Instead, humbly come to the Lord, thank Him for His faithfulness, and trust His timing.

"Therefore humble yourselves under the mighty hand of God, that He may exalt you in due time..."
– 1 Peter 5:6

Many of us attempt to exalt ourselves instead of trusting that we will be exalted by God in due time if we persist in humility. The problem comes when we "play God" through self-promotion instead of choosing humility, coming in low, and patiently waiting to be lifted up in the Lord's timing.

Jesus affirms this idea in the Sermon on the Mount. He explains that the Kingdom works counter-intuitively to worldly logic. The poor are made rich, the mourners are comforted, and the meek inherit the earth! Those in a lowly place are exalted by the Lord, while those who are currently exalted are humbled by Jesus' sobering "woes" (see Luke 6:24-26).

In the book of James, the believer is challenged to wait for God's hand to exalt the lowly: "Let the lowly brother glory in his exaltation, but the rich in his humiliation" (James 1:9-10). It is clear that the solution to our battle with pride is a heart postured in humility.

Humility is the Fear of the Lord

Humility is not a mysterious core value that eludes us whenever we seek to obtain it. It is actually clearly defined in Proverbs.

"Humility is the fear of the Lord,
its wages are riches, honor and life."
– Proverbs 22:4 NIV

To fear the Lord is to honor, revere, and acknowledge the sovereign authority of our Lord and Creator. His Word is eternal. He is the Uncreated One. To walk in the fear of the Lord requires us to submit, knowing His ways are higher than our own (see Is. 55:8-9). The fear of the Lord is a keen awareness of God's holiness. Anyone who fears the Lord has a healthy understanding that God hates sin and all the enemy is doing on the earth. Proverbs 8 gives us a straightforward definition: "The fear of the Lord is to hate evil."

Why am I emphasizing this so heavily? I believe that the majority of Christians have taken a massive step away from a healthy reverence of God and hatred of sin. We have become complacent with the "little foxes that spoil the vines" (Song of Sol. 2:15) instead of understanding that "the fear of the Lord is the beginning of knowledge" (Prov. 1:7). This is how God introduces humility to us. It is a lifestyle of despising sin and honoring His Word above all things, including our perception of our experiences. Our entire lives are humbled at the realization that we can do absolutely nothing to save ourselves from the very power of pride that God *hates.*

"We were by nature deserving of wrath. But because of his great love for us, God, who is rich in mercy, made us alive with Christ even when we were dead in transgressions— it is by grace you have been saved...through faith— and this is not from yourselves, it is the gift of God— not by works, so that no one can boast."
– Ephesians 2:3-5, 9 NIV

Instead of giving us the wrath and punishment we deserved, God lovingly chose to have mercy. He saved you by grace—a gift that comes through faith! You cannot boast about or claim any responsibility for the salvation you have received. Humility is the foundation and is deeply connected to all of this. It is a heart posture you must possess.

Whenever I minister, a common question I ask is, "What stops most believers from stepping into the call of God on their lives?" Usually, people respond by calling out different ideas: Fear. Shame. Distraction. Busyness. Comfort. Lack. Sin. Pain. Whatever reason they give, it always ties back to one common denominator: *me. My* shame, *my* busyness, *my* comfort. We tend to be the biggest obstacle to God's work in and through us. We frequently get in the way due to prideful thinking and behavior. We twist the Gospel into something chiefly self-beneficial instead of seeing that it truly is about Jesus and the demonstration of His selfless love through our lives.

If you were honest with yourself, you'd know you could not be righteous on your own. You don't need to be afraid of taking off the mask of pride and performance. You are not going to be punished because you have already been changed into a new man or woman. Condemnation is gone, fear is unnecessary, and pride was unattractive to begin with. Pastor Eric Johnson says it like this, "Without Christ, you are nothing. With Him, you are everything."

This is the exact realization one of the leaders on my team came to understand. He was consumed with his own abilities and talents and lost sight of the One who had designed him with the very gifts he was boasting in. It was only once his heart was softened and humbled by God's love that his life took on a brand new edge with even greater potential than before.

James' Story

Growing up, I always believed that maturity was the absence of need. I thought only "weak" people needed others and that if I could take care of myself I would be content. I had bought into the lie that full-blown independence is healthy, entertaining beliefs such as, "Be your own man, create your own path, prove yourself, and be strong and succeed at any cost." It did not occur to me that this thinking would lay the groundwork for a lifestyle of pride. As I grew up in the Christian world, I observed and imitated the cultural tendency to hide weakness while displaying strength, achievement, and success. When I began struggling with habitual sin, I frantically covered it up with an array of achievements. I was terrified of someone finding out how badly I really was struggling. I believed that my value was contingent on my performance, and my worth was determined by my external image. I had to hide to survive. If I shoved my struggles down where no one could see them, I was safe. If people saw who I really was and what I struggled with, they would find me disgusting and unlovable.

When I applied to Grace Place discipleship housing, the application was filled with questions about my weaknesses and struggles—not the questions I was used to on a traditional college or job application. I wrote extensively, enhancing my positive characteristics and using well-worded language to conceal any obvious flaws. I thought these were the answers needed to "get me in." I had an interview with Daniel, the founder of Grace Place. He brought up a huge inconsistency with my entire application: "James, this all seems too good to be true." He started asking questions that revealed the truth, and it scared me to death. Daniel could see right through my mask. "Why do you feel the need to make things seem better than they are?" he asked me. Somewhere behind all my smoke and mirrors hid a scared, hurting boy, petrified of being condemned and rejected. As the video interview came to a close, Daniel looked me in the eyes and said, "James, I don't feel like this program is going to be a good fit for you if this is how you handle the reality of your life." He denied me, and that was the end of my interview.

I couldn't believe it. I thought, "This is ridiculous. He must have an impossible standard. If I'm not acceptable, how could anyone be?" But behind the frustration, I knew he was right. Daniel saw a piece of me I hadn't allowed anyone to see. While I was more aware than ever of my struggle with sin, tendency to hide, and performance-based mindset, I was also experiencing something I had long forgotten: hope. In the face of apparent rejection, I began believing that freedom was possible. Perhaps beyond my self-constructed prison of pride was someone who could help me be free.

After texting him, Daniel was willing to meet with me again. I started by confessing, "Daniel, you are right. I'm in a mess and I need help. I don't deserve to be in your discipleship program, and I certainly don't walk in a godly standard of integrity and purity in my life. I've always tried to hide my flaws, and that is wrong. Will you please re-consider allowing me to join this program?" We sat in silence until Daniel responded, "James, I'd like to pray about it. We'll let you know within the week what we decide."

I will never forget receiving that call. Daniel's familiar voice was on the other end of the line: "James, I just wanted to let you know that we've prayed about it, and we feel that you would be the perfect fit for this program. Welcome to Grace Place." I was shocked. What had changed? I certainly hadn't improved morally.

A few months into my first year under Daniel's mentorship, I asked him, "Why did you change your mind about me?" He told me, "James, when I look at applications for Grace Place, I am looking at three key characteristics: humility, teachability, and potential. When you applied, it was abundantly clear that you had potential—through the roof! But pride was keeping you from seeing where you were at. I would rather have one humble applicant with seemingly 'low' potential than ten high-potential ones who walk in pride or arrogance. When you asked to meet again and admitted that you were in a mess and needed help, that's when I knew you were ready to be discipled."

Sadly, I had been wearing a mask for most of my life, and I was never able to receive love from God or from others. Any encouragement or attempt to show love bounced right off. My subconscious would accuse, "They don't really love you. They don't see what's really going on. If they knew, they could never love you that way." It was only when, in the middle of my biggest messes, I chose humility and honesty that transformation occurred. Once I was shown love and forgiveness when I didn't deserve it, my mind understood that God could also be like this.

I learned to take down the mask and choose blunt honesty, and the love that was shown to me penetrated my heart and opened my eyes to see that, even at my worst, I was loved.

Honesty requires humility. It is the antithesis of pride because it openly admits, "I cannot. But God, You can. Please help me." When there is nothing in the dark, I have nothing to hide and nothing can condemn me because there is nothing that remains "unknown." Freedom from pride began that day. I know I only have one job—to come before the Lord honestly and humbly, with nothing hidden. I can come to Him in my weakness, knowing that in my weakness, He is strong. When I am at the end of myself, He begins.

Chapter Five

Condemnation and Righteousness

Condemnation is often misunderstood. People can easily tell you what fear and pride are, but you will find many at a loss for words when asked to describe "condemnation." So what is condemnation?

The root word of condemnation used in Scripture is translated from the Greek word *katakrima* which means "to pass sentence, judge worthy of punishment, or judge someone as guilty; a damnatory sentence." To receive condemnation is to receive a sentence saying that you are damned or worthy of punishment.

Now, practically speaking, no one is going around sentencing you to death on a daily basis. Condemnation happens within. It's an internal war that fights to bring you down. It's the voice inside your head that leaves you feeling guilty, ashamed, and worthless. The moment you stumble, think a bad thought, or fall short of perfection, condemnation lurks at the door waiting to pounce.

"Death once held us in its grip, and by the blunder of one man, death reigned as king over humanity. But now, how much more are we held in the grip of grace and continue reigning as kings in life, enjoying our regal freedom through the gift of perfect righteousness in the one and only Jesus, the Messiah! In other words, just as condemnation came upon all people through one transgression, so through one righteous act of Jesus' sacrifice, the perfect righteousness that makes us right with God and leads us to a victorious life is now available to all."

– Romans 5:17-18 TPT

Condemnation brings death. Think of a house or building that's been "condemned." What's going to happen to it? It's going to be destroyed. It's not suitable to be lived in. The demolition crew marks it with bright hazard tape, warning the world of it's coming demise. It's dangerous, and it could collapse at any given moment.

At times, we can feel this way about ourselves. If we lose sight of our value, the demolitioner (the devil) gives us all the reasons we aren't worthy to be a son or daughter. He nags us with our flaws and insufficiencies. "Jesus doesn't want to live inside of you. You look like you're about to crumble. That sin you committed last night is unforgivable. Just give up! How can the Holy Spirit stay here!?"

However, what does Jesus do? Revelation 3:20 says He comes and knocks on the door of your heart, so He might come in and dine with you. Who would go and have dinner in a house that's about to collapse? Who would choose you even when you're in the midst of feeling completely worthless? Jesus. And not only does He come inside, but He also restores you, redeems you, and makes you brand new.

The demolitioner can only come when there is an adequate reason for destruction. So on what basis does the devil have a right to condemn us? Well, he doesn't. Not anymore.

In the Old Testament, sin was the gateway for condemnation. If you sinned and there was no sacrifice given, then you reaped the reward of your blunder. "The wages of sin is death..." (Rom. 6:23). If you work as a sinner, your salary is paid to you in condemnation. You get what you deserve.

According to the law, if there is even a trace of sin in your life, condemnation has legal access. However, if there is no sin present, there is no right for condemnation and death to enter in. So it comes down to this. Is sin present within you? Are you worthy of being condemned?

Great question.

When the Law and commandments came through Moses, sin was imputed to everyone under the system. "Imputed" is a legal term meaning "to ascribe to or charge (a person) with an act or quality because of the conduct of another." Mankind has been receiving death not just because of each individual's sins but because of the sin of Adam. The Bible shows that man is born into sin, reaping the sentence for Adam's transgression. The only one who was not born into sin was Jesus, because He came through the virgin birth.

"He who does not believe is condemned already, because he has not believed in the name of the only begotten Son of God."
–John 3:18

So to answer the question: Yes. According to the Old Covenant, you are worthy of condemnation. Why? Because you were born into sin. All of us were. Condemnation is our default setting. Sin has entangled itself into our nature. It has decayed humanity into a housing scheme of collapsing structures, all of which are unsuitable for occupation. So then the question is: *Why does Jesus STILL want to live inside of me?*

The Sinless One

Jesus became sin. He was born without a speck of it. He lived a blameless life. There was not a single accusation that could be rightly thrown at Him. He was perfect. Yet He chose to become the embodiment of your faults. He absorbed the sins of humanity into Himself and experienced the condemnation we all deserve. Scripture says He went into the depths of hell itself (see Eph. 4:9). Why? So you wouldn't have to. Jesus became what you were so you could become who He is.

While you rightly deserve the demolition due for your sin, Jesus rewrote the policy. He flipped everything upside down. He has washed you of your sins and made you holy. You are no longer a sinner, but a son or daughter of a Heavenly Father. Jesus took what the world saw as worthless and called you by a new name: a house fit for a king.

How to Deal with Condemnation

While the Bible is clear on the subject of condemnation, we Christians generally do not understand the negative effects that feelings of condemnation have on our lives. This ignorance allows the enemy to have a heyday with our minds. Condemnation comes to stifle us and make us ineffective. It does everything it can to separate you from God. It's like a hamster wheel that's always demanding you run a little harder and a little faster to make up for your mistakes, but it never takes you anywhere.

We feel the need to perform under the heavy weight of condemnation because we *forget to remember*. What does that mean? We forget to remember the sacrifice that has already been paid! We lose sight of our communion with the spotless Lamb of God who has *already* performed, finished, and supplied everything we will ever need for life and godliness (see 2 Peter 1:3)! Condemnation comes to take your eyes off of His blood, sweat, and tears and onto your own. *What can you do? How can you make up for your actions? What are you doing today to be more holy?*

When we recognize the Cross of Jesus Christ and hold it in our remembrance, condemnation's voice grows dim! If we lose sight of our blood-washed reality, condemnation will slither its way back in and try to befriend us with deceptions of "hard work" and "holy sacrificial acts."

It reminds me of an experience that one of the leaders in my ministry went through. As you connect with her story, allow her victory to be your own. As you read, take hold of this important truth: condemnation is NOT from God!

Katherine's Story

We were debriefing as a team after another great day of ministry on the East Coast. We had ministered at a service in Pennsylvania earlier that day and I had an unusual experience during the worship time. I was feeling all sorts of emotions, had racing and random thoughts going through my mind, and wondered if God heard me or was near.

In our debrief, Daniel mentioned how much spiritual warfare was going on in that church. We talked about it as a team and went through many different occurrences that pointed out the presence of the demonic in the service. I felt prompted to share the experience I had in worship, and Daniel helped me see that what I was experiencing was actually discernment, not my own struggle. I was shocked because this seemed to go against my understanding of God. I believed He wanted to highlight my issues in times of connection with Him, such as worship. I thought this was the sign of a good relationship with God–that He would always be bringing up things I needed to work on with Him.

The team helped me understand that the negative feelings and thoughts I had in this corporate setting were not things I normally struggled with. What I had identified as my own struggle was actually the result of heightened spiritual awareness. I blurted out, "But I thought if God didn't highlight my issues in my time with Him, I wasn't having a good time with Him!" Members of the team were shocked, and I sat back in silence, thinking of what all this could mean. After the debrief was over, I ran to my room and immediately started to cry–wail, actually. I had never experienced this type of crying before.

My mentor, Annie, held me in her arms as I released a cry of freedom. I let go of the feeling of condemnation and not being good enough before God. I let go of the obsessive focus on my failures and the need to fix myself. I let go of the lies that told me God was a taskmaster that expected perfection of me without helping me get there. I began to realize that He really just wanted to be with me, and He loved me the way I was. I realized that I did not need to continue to analyze myself because Jesus had already paid the price for me to stand in His presence, blameless and pure. Jesus was the perfect sacrifice, so I do not need to be. What He has done for me is enough!

This is amazing! How many of us find ourselves in the exact same spot as Katherine? "I thought if God didn't highlight my issues in my time with Him, I wasn't having a good time with Him!" The truth is exactly as she said: when we recognize Jesus is the sacrifice, we realize we don't need to punish ourselves! You don't ever need to feel condemned in His presence! Certainly, there are times to repent and change the way you think, but repentance doesn't feel like guilt, shame, and condemnation. It feels like being raw, open, and true before Jesus, with the full knowledge that you're loved and will never be punished by Him!

"I [have] sworn that I would not be angry with you, nor rebuke you. For the mountains shall depart and the hills be removed, but My kindness shall not depart from you, nor shall My covenant of peace be removed,' says the Lord, who has mercy on you."
– Isaiah 54:9-10

This scripture makes it clear that God is no longer angry with us. Why can't we believe this? Why can't we take Him at His word? Condemnation is a liar. We must always remember His promises, His sacrifice, and His unfailing love—especially when we are confronted with the condemning voice of the wicked one. This is why reading the Word is so important. Scripture reminds us who we are!

The Voice of The Accuser

"Now whom you forgive anything, I also forgive. For if indeed I have forgiven anything, I have forgiven that one for your sakes in the presence of Christ, lest Satan should take advantage of us; for we are not ignorant of his devices."
– 2 Corinthians 2:10-11

The word "satan" means "adversary, opposer, one to accuse or question." The book of Revelation calls our enemy the "accuser of the brethren and the one who deceives the whole world" (see Rev. 12:9-10). Paul tells us to be aware of the tactics of the enemy. His purpose is to bring accusation and to act as an attorney of the law against mankind.

Anyone that has been involved in my ministry for more than a few days has heard me say the phrase, "all things." This is in reference to Philippians 4:13 and Romans 8:28. I have seen the truth of these two Scriptures reveal itself repeatedly throughout my life. It seems that very frequently, I or someone on my leadership team in Grace Place has a story of how something went wrong, but the Lord worked it together for good. If someone says they can't do something, I respond with "You can do all things" because it reminds them of what they're capable of in Christ.

We can do all things through Christ who strengthens us, and the enemy knows he is powerless in stopping the Christian who takes this verse to heart. So what does he do? He attempts to clip your wings by convincing you that you are powerless. He uses lies of condemnation to deceive us into believing that we have been, and always will be, ineffective in the Kingdom. He knows that you will not be able to do "all things" if you identify with your mistakes and believe you are unable to overcome them.

God wants you to realize that you are uncondemned and righteous by faith so that He can use you. We often say, "God, we are your vessels!" but then we turn around and say that we cannot do all things. Is Christ in you strong enough to accomplish anything? Then let go of the discouragement that is fueled by feelings of condemnation and start believing the truth!

Condemnation vs. Consequence

Condemnation leaves us in a constant state of believing that punishment is coming our way. I'm not saying that there are no consequences for our actions. If you speed through a red light, there's a high chance of collision with another car. However, God wouldn't be responsible for wrecking your car. You would be. You broke the traffic law!

However, even in an example like this, there is still no condemnation for us from God. We are in Christ, forever sealed by the blood. Responsibility does need to be taken for the wrong committed, and sometimes natural consequences can occur. However, that doesn't mean God is punishing you!

When you take responsibility, you come in low, humbly admitting your fault. "God opposes the proud, but gives grace to the humble" (1 Peter 5:5). When you respond in humility, being honest about your sin, how would He not come through in mercy and work it together for your good? Condemnation is a punishment that removes hope of redemption or reconciliation, directly in defiance of the Gospel.

Even when you do face the earthly consequences of your sin, you don't have to do it alone. You aren't separated from God or left to fend for yourself. He is intimately interested in walking through any difficulty with you, offering His unconditional love, forgiveness, and reassurance that He will never forsake you.

It's when we get condemned *by* the consequences that we get really trapped! What does that look like? It's when you make a mistake and then decide that you *are* the consequences of your actions. *I wrecked my car... so I'm a wreck!*

Regardless of how much of a mess you make, you are loved—deeply loved. God does not lock you into your consequences. I've seen God supernaturally heal people from diseases caused by overeating, smoking, drug abuse, reckless living, etc. He never leaves people labeled by their *cause*. He loves them just the same as though they never fell. He restores them according to their identity and not according to what they deserve.

Whether consequences come from something you've done intentionally, because of a lack of knowledge, or by a complete accident, you are loved, you are cherished, and you are not condemned!

Condemnation in Relationships

Condemnation tries to seep in anywhere that we have missed the mark. One of the places the enemy wreaks havoc is in relationships. I have walked many of the people I disciple through reconciliation with their families and friends. A predominant lie that the enemy condemns people with is, "Because you made a mistake in the relationship, you can never recover, and this relationship will always be broken." *Nonsense*! This could not be farther from the truth.

"Blessed are the peacemakers,
For they shall be called sons of God."
– Matthew 5:9

Jesus did not say, "Blessed are the peace*keepers*," He said, "Blessed are the peace*makers*." He came to turn son against father and daughter against mother (see Luke 12:53). He was not interested in "keeping the peace," but He was set on making true peace. Relationships frequently have disagreements and disputes. If you feel condemned and believe that your (or others') mistakes spell the end of your relationships, then you will have few long-lasting relationships. The relationships you will have are likely to be shallow in areas that you disagree.

Those who are immature and feel condemned for how they have failed in relationships believe that arguments mean the end of the relationship. Those who are mature and uncondemned know that disagreements only breed deeper relationships through reconciliation. The majority of the people closest to me are the people that I have had the most disagreements with. When you are in ministry, you deal with people doing painful things to you all the time. I cannot tell you the number of times that someone I am discipling has broken my trust and done something hurtful.

When they make mistakes, intentionally or not, we resolve the issues by talking about what they did or did not do and discussing how that has affected our relationship. However, I never hold on to their wrongdoings or allow them to shape how I view them. No matter how rough the circumstance may be (and trust me, there have been many hurtful ones), I never allow myself to entertain the thought that the argument or offense could end the relationship. Instead, I forgive them, and we move on to be closer than we were before. A relationship under the law is condemned to fail because it reaps what is sown. A wrong committed is a wrong returned. However, a relationship under grace is destined to succeed through forgiveness.

Disputes or disagreements can be like breaking a bone. When we have an argument, the relationship can feel tense or heated. In the same way, when you break a bone there is an immediate flow of blood to the injury, resulting in swelling and bruising. However, when blood flows to the site of the broken bone, it begins the process of healing. When that bone is finally healed, it is stronger than it was before the injury. It is extremely unlikely that this bone will be broken in the same place again.

Eventually, the body eats away at the bone's callous and it returns to the original shape, making it difficult to discern that there had ever been a break at all. We can look at a relationship in the moment of a fight or friction and think to ourselves, *Ah! This is bad. Everything seems inflamed.* However, we must take a moment to see the big picture and remember that healing will take place under the surface.

"There is therefore now no condemnation to those who are in Christ Jesus..."
– Romans 8:1

Condemnation assures us of doom in whatever area it affects, but it is a lie. Any time you feel that a positive outcome is hopeless due to your own failure, condemnation is at work. The devil has brought an accusation against you and tried to convince you that you will reap the effects of your failure. However, God has justified you through your belief in Jesus. You are no longer accusable! When you realize you are free from condemnation, you will begin to see that God is for you and not against you. With Him, all things are possible.

There's No Need to Hide

Over the years, I have often seen those I disciple go through cycles of sin, condemnation, and isolation. First, they sin and defile their consciences. Then, because they do not understand the love and grace of God, they feel condemned. After they accept condemnation as reality, they tend to hide from God, myself, and those around them. They run to isolation because they do not want to suffer the punishment they believe they deserve. Even if the mess was small, I can sense them start to disconnect and hide.

I know something's up when someone can't look me in the eyes. Isolation traps you in deception because you are hiding from the light. Sin stored away in secrecy always breeds more and more misconceptions of who God really is toward you. The weight of condemnation grows heavier the longer you remain in the shadows. An invisible barrier is built and you create an imaginary force field between you, God, and those around you.

However, when you recognize that you won't be punished for your faults, failures, and misunderstandings, it's easy to come out of hiding! The moment you step into the light is the moment you can receive love from God despite your mistakes! Remember what the Word of God says: "[*nothing*] shall be able to separate us from the love of God which is in Christ Jesus our Lord" (Rom. 8:39).

Check out the story below. A member of my team realized how pointless it was to hide and experienced God's loving embrace by stepping into the light. Many of us can relate to wanting to hide, but when you know you're loved, there's never a reason to keep your distance!

Phillip's Story

A couple of years ago, I had a time when I was dealing with a pornography addiction. I could go a few weeks maintaining my purity, but then I would feel tempted and fall back into looking at porn. I would feel so condemned because all the voices in my head said, "You'll never be able to get married now!" Or, "If anyone knew about what you just did, they would become so frustrated with you, judge you, and ultimately reject you."

Luckily, I had a leader in my life, Daniel, who did not quit on me and never let my past mistakes affect how he viewed me. I remember it all came to a head when I fell back into a cycle of choosing pornography and decided I was a lost cause. I went about cutting off everyone in my life: my family, my friends, my housemates, and the leaders in my life, including Daniel. I avoided all types of communication and when asked in person if I was ok, I would lie and respond with "I'm doing ok," or, "I'm fine." All the while I was deeply hurting on the inside. I was dealing with condemnation, thinking that God was so disappointed with me and that I was unredeemable.

The weight of condemnation was hanging over me every moment of my day. I felt this way until I had a run-in with the truth. One night, Daniel came over to my house and talked to me about the truth of the Gospel. I learned about His blood being shed for me on the Cross in order for me to have true intimacy with my Heavenly Father. Jesus had already dealt with my condemnation at the Cross!

That night I stepped into the light and allowed the truth to break in, even though I was afraid of being humiliated and shamed for my sins. I was met with love. I was met with grace! Daniel didn't condemn me for my faults, and neither did God! I discovered all over again, according to Romans 8:1, "There is therefore now no condemnation for those who are in Christ Jesus." This truth helped me overcome the weight of condemnation and I began to walk in freedom.

The Difference Between Conviction and Condemnation

Phillip didn't need a fresh wind of condemnation to get him out of his sins. He needed a fresh wind of conviction to propel him toward his God-given identity! He stepped into the light, and from that place, he was able to see who God truly is toward him. "For with You is the fountain of life; in Your light we see light" (Ps. 36:9).

We need to identify the voice of the accuser so that we can differentiate between the voice of condemnation (which brings death) and the voice of the Holy Spirit's conviction (which brings life). As we live in relationship with the Holy Spirit, He will convict us when we do things that do not line up with His Word and our identity in Him. The Holy Spirit is our Helper, and He is with us in every moment in every place. His conviction is what brings us to maturity.

"Nevertheless I tell you the truth. It is to your advantage that I go away; for if I do not go away, the Helper will not come to you; but if I depart, I will send Him to you. And when He has come, He will convict the world of sin, and of righteousness, and of judgment: of sin, because they do not believe in Me; of righteousness, because I go to My Father and you see Me no more; of judgment, because the ruler of this world is judged."

—John 16:8-11

The role of the Holy Spirit is the conviction of sin, righteousness, and judgment. Notice that it says "sin," not "sins." Singular, not plural. The key is *what* singular sin is being convicted. The Holy Spirit convicts the world of their sin of *unbelief* in Jesus. All of the sins (plural) come from the sin (singular) of unbelief.

However, if you do believe in Jesus, He is not convicting you of sin, but rather of righteousness. It's conviction of righteousness that brings repentance. One simple way to determine whether it is the Holy Spirit convicting you or the enemy accusing you is to see where your focus is drawn.

Conviction is focused on *God*: "God is calling me to a higher standard." Condemnation is focused on *me*: "I should have done something better." When you hear the voice of conviction, you are inspired to manifest righteousness. No matter how deep our sin, conviction brings us to the realization that, through Christ, there is redemption.

"Woe is me, for I am undone! Because I am a man of unclean lips, And I dwell in the midst of a people of unclean lips; For my eyes have seen the King, The Lord of hosts."
– Isaiah 6:5

The conviction of the Holy Spirit shows you the stark wickedness of your sin against the contrast of the pure goodness of God, leaving you in awe of Him. His voice leaves you hope-filled in awareness of the possibilities of living righteously. Instead of being met with the harsh standard of the law, you are filled with God's grace and empowered to change. You have to understand the difference between conviction and condemnation; otherwise, you will keep living in a downward spiral of repetitive failure.

I am convinced that the devil masquerades himself as the Holy Spirit convicting believers of sin. In reality, he is the accuser of the brethren, releasing guilt, shame, and condemnation on people. Often, the enemy overplays his hand. If his lies were projected on a screen in front of you, they would be laughable. Yet, in the hidden places of our minds, they feel very real. This is why it's so important that we tune our hearts to the Spirit's voice and expose the lies of condemnation for what they are—false! If it's not life-giving, it's not Him.

True conviction from the Holy Spirit leads to repentance. It is God calling us to a higher standard. Condemnation leads to self-focus and sin-consciousness. I find that those who feel convicted dwell on their mistakes for a short amount of time, but those under the influence of the voice of condemnation become consumed with their shortcomings. Condemnation and conviction are two different voices, and we need to know the difference!

"Search me, O God, and know my heart;
Try me, and know my anxieties;
And see if there is any wicked way in me,
And lead me in the way everlasting."
– Psalm 139:23-24

Conviction comes through relationship. When religion and the law are present in the way we think, we constantly focus on ourselves and our sin. We try to make ourselves perfect by correcting our actions. God is not concerned with our ability to improve our behavior. He is concerned with our hearts. Conviction is one of the most precious parts of being a believer. I have experienced conviction that leaves me in tears and a conviction that sends me into laughter. It all comes through hearing His voice within the context of relationship. In the

Bible, David did not search his own heart to find how he could improve himself in order to please God. He asked *God* to search his heart (see Ps. 139:23). If you feel like something is off in your life, don't go digging to try and find where it's coming from. Instead, ask God to search your heart. He will show you anything you may be overlooking.

While mentoring and discipling, I have discovered one reliable way to determine whether someone is under the voice of conviction or condemnation is: watch how he or she responds when confronted. When we listen to the voice of conviction, humility is produced in our hearts. We are inspired to pursue relationships with God and leaders in order to change and grow. On the flip side, a condemned believer often responds in one of two ways. They either appear inwardly focused and hopeless of ever living in victory over sin, or they respond in pride, defending their every action and occasionally putting down others in the process.

When I confront those living in pride, I often find it necessary to respond very directly to their defensive attitude. You might say, "Well, that doesn't sound like love," but Jesus called the Pharisees a brood of vipers and constantly responded harshly to them. I'm not afraid to be direct with someone who is acting defensively, but I always respond in compassion when I have broken through the mask of pride. I understand that the only reason they were prideful in the first place was because they were afraid of being condemned and are resistant to correction.

Take a look at the table below to get an idea of what the voice of condemnation sounds like versus the voice of conviction. This, of course, isn't written in stone. There are an infinite number of intricate scenarios you could be faced with. Your relationship with the Spirit will allow you to rightly discern between the voices of guilt and love.

CONDEMNATION	CONVICTION
I can't believe I did that... I'm such a failure.	*I shouldn't have done that... Father, thank you for loving me even now. Please help me and empower me to walk in righteousness.*
I keep making the same mistake. I'm such a mess. How will I ever escape this cycle?	*I did it again. I'm sorry Father. I'm stuck in this cycle and I can't break it in my own strength. Please empower me, Holy Spirit. Dress me in Your robes of righteousness.*
Maybe if I just work harder, supress my feelings, and become numb to my emotions, I can be better!	*I open myself to you, Father. Search me and know me. Here are my emotions, my feelings, my sins. Please wash me with your Word!*
I have that sinking feeling of pressure and anxiety in my chest.	*God, I feel heavy-laden. I choose to cast my cares on You. I know that You love me. Please show me that love. Let me experience it again.*
I have swirling accusations and judgements in my head.	*Father, my mind is a war zone. I choose your Word over the accusations. I choose forgiveness over guilt. I receive the truth that sets me free!*

Walking Free From Condemnation

As you can see from the table, the voice of condemnation only makes you more aware of your failures. Condemnation is evidence of living under the law. It is the result of not believing the truth of God's redemption and your born again nature in Christ. When you feel condemned, you will walk in fear, you will operate in pride, and guilt and shame will plague your thoughts. Condemnation is the opposite of freedom. Do you believe that God has more for you than being trapped by the lie that you are not "good enough?" I believe so, and my main goal is that you would clearly see your new identity in Him. If you can see it, you will start to believe it and experience it. Remember, it is knowing the truth that sets you free! Condemnation has just as much of a place in your life as hell: none whatsoever!

God has a beautiful plan for every aspect of our lives. When we live in grace and remain uncondemned, we live a life with no limitations, filled with love, joy, peace, patience, kindness, goodness, faithfulness, gentleness, and self-control (see Gal. 5:22-23). Steward an awareness of His voice in your heart. Learn what He sounds like. Pray prayers like, "Soften my heart, Lord, to hear your voice in every area of my life. I want to know you." A sure way to cultivate His Word in your heart is to meditate on His words toward you. Remember, because you are justified by faith in Christ Jesus, "you are not under law but under grace" (Rom. 6:14). The next time you feel accusations arise in your mind or emotions, I want you to remember this passage:

"Who then would dare to accuse those whom God has chosen in love to be his? God Himself is the judge who has issued His final verdict over them—'Not guilty!' Who then is left to condemn us? Certainly not Jesus, the Anointed One! For He gave His life for us, and even more than that, He has conquered death and is now risen, exalted, and enthroned by God at His right hand. So how could He possibly condemn us since He is continually praying for our triumph? Who could ever separate us from the endless love of God's Anointed One? Absolutely no one! For nothing in the universe has the power to diminish His love toward us. Troubles, pressures, and problems are unable to come between us and heaven's love. What about persecutions, deprivations, dangers, and death threats? No, for they are all impotent to hinder omnipotent love..."

– Romans 8:33-35 TPT

Chapter Six

The Finished Work

Growing up in a conservative Christian school, I frequently heard the foundational teaching of man's sinful nature. The majority of the students and faculty, like the contemporary Christian Church as a whole, held to the belief that we are nothing more than evil, wicked sinners, saved by grace. Ironically, as I grew up at my Word of Faith charismatic church, I was taught a different perspective: that we are amazing, powerful, awesome "world-changers." At some point, these two extremes needed to be reconciled in my mind, and the key difference was more subtle than I thought. My school was not wrong. My church was not wrong. Both of these statements, though they seem to conflict, are mostly true.

It is the Cross that makes the difference—the key distinction between sinner and saint is the co-crucifixion and co-resurrection with Christ that happens at salvation. We are buried with Christ as sinners and are raised up as born-again sons of God. The Cross is the determining factor. At Calvary, mankind in all his sinfulness was terminated.

"I have been crucified with Christ; it is no longer I who live, but Christ lives in me; and the life which I now live in the flesh I live by faith in the Son of God, who loved me and gave Himself for me."
– Galatians 2:20

I was a wicked sinner. However, I am now a righteous son of God, adopted and redeemed. Everything broken, sinful, and diseased was placed on Christ at the Cross. He took my place and embraced the death I deserved. This is a critical distinction to make: the old me is dead, and I am now living as a new creation with the Spirit of Christ inside of me. My nature has been changed, and sin has been defeated. If you do not believe this, you will always think there is an internal battle occurring between a sinful nature and a love for God, when the entire purpose of Christ's incarnation was to destroy sin. 1 John 3:8 clearly states, "For this purpose the Son of God was manifested, that He might destroy the works of the devil."

Sin is the enemy. It disfigures, deceives, and distorts man's original purpose. Christ came not to judge sinners, but to become sin itself, to die as it, and to take upon Himself the very judgment of God. The problem of sin had to be dealt with; otherwise, we could never be victorious. Without the Cross, we are left no better than where we started—as broken humans doing their best to fix themselves in a never-ending cycle.

The True Enemy

We know that sin is a deeply-rooted problem that has infected every man and woman since the garden of Eden. All humans are born with a sin nature that is entirely ego-centric. We defend and bring value to ourselves in an entitled and prideful way. Everything is about me, me, me. *What's in it for me? Don't forget me. That's offensive to me. Stop getting in my way. You are making me late.* We even go so far as to think, *If I do this, what's God gonna do for me?*

Pastor Eric Johnson from Greenville, SC calls this type of self-focus "me-ology." Meology is one of the greatest problems in the world today. While it is dressed up to look beneficial, it is actually just sinfulness in disguise. Manipulation, corruption, bribery, and all the rest stem from sin. Most everything that you have experienced outside of the fulfilling life Jesus promised comes back to fear, pride, and condemnation, which are byproducts of a sin nature.

The issue is taken a step further when we consider that we not only struggle with sin's trappings but also lack knowledge of the truth. People everywhere are born into this problem of sin and do not even understand that there is a solution. The good news is that we are not without hope. The Church is continuously growing in her understanding of the finished work, and she is gaining momentum as she discovers her new creation reality.

The Cross declares the Father's heart toward humanity, and we cannot become complacent with our current level of understanding. We must continue to pursue the truth. So much more was made available than we think we know! Scripture sums up these concepts powerfully. Romans 5:18 describes not only our universal problem but also the universal solution:

"Therefore, as through one man's offense judgment came to all men, resulting in condemnation, even so through one Man's righteous act the free gift came to all men, resulting in justification of life."

– Romans 5:18

The righteous "Man" from Romans 5:18 is the Son of Man. The Gospel was and always will be focused on this universal solution: Jesus Christ. The answer lies in Him, not us! We need to get over ourselves! The Gospel was never about us. It's about what Christ has done. We are merely a conduit who God chooses to use, a dwelling place for His love and power. It is not about our ability or strength. It is about Him working through us.

Until you believe in the power of the Gospel, you won't live in the fullness of what Jesus paid for. God Almighty, the Creator of the universe, sent His Son because He considered Himself rich to have us in His family. His finished work, not our own efforts, sets us free from sin. The counterintuitive truth is that the less we focus on our flaws and the more we focus on His accomplishment, the freer we become. Jesus paid for you to be free. He wants you to walk in freedom and victory, not just from fear, pride, and condemnation, but from sin and self. Do you believe that?

Stop It

At this point, you can hopefully see that our old identity operated under the dangerous standard of "You *are* what you *do*." If we continue to live with that belief, we will never live in freedom. The beauty of being a new creation in Christ is that we are no longer identified by our actions. We are no longer sinners! We are saints and sons, not because we deserve it or because we have behaved correctly, but because of the position we stand in: covered by Jesus' blood. I am constantly reminding people, "You are not who your feelings say you are," "You are not who your actions say you are," and "You are not who your past says you are." You are who *God* says you are. That is the liberty of believing the truth and allowing it to set you free (see John 8:32). You are a *believer,* not a *feeler.*

Beyond the misunderstanding of your identity, people also read conflict and separation into their relationship with God because of their sin, shortcomings, or shame. However, in reality, there is no separation, even after stumbling or sinning. Jesus' purpose was to bridge the unclosable gap by coming in our place to die the death we deserved so we could walk in the life He deserved. The life Jesus deserves is a life of full, uninterrupted connection with the Father, unhindered by fear, pride, or condemnation.

If you were Jesus Himself, would you have any difficulty believing that God is pleased with you, that He wants to have a relationship with you, or that He is constantly working on your behalf? Of course not! What about you? Do you believe God is 100% pleased with you? Do you think He wants a continuous relationship with you? Are you convinced He is always working for your good and never against you? If you answered "no" to any of these questions, it is an indicator that you are seeing yourself as separate from Christ. As previously mentioned, the solution is simple: STOP IT. There is no need for a long, drawn-out process. Simply change the way you think!

When you order a package, there is a processing time you expect in order to receive your package. Do not treat your understanding of the Gospel in this same way. We think we need to send up a prayer to ask for God's help with our current sin issue, and we expect that we will have to wait for an encounter or some life-changing moment. But God has already finished the work. There is no shipping and processing time. He already took us through the process. He pulled us out of the domain of darkness and put us into the Kingdom of the Son that He loves (see Col. 1:13). In fact, this package has already been signed, sealed, and delivered... signed in the blood of Jesus, sealed by the Holy Spirit, and delivered to us by grace through faith.

So STOP IT! Stop struggling with your sin. It's not yours any longer. Stop wallowing in your failures and mistakes. You are not the prodigal son anymore. You are clothed in His righteousness, empowered by His Spirit, and seated in His household forever. You are DEAD. He is ALIVE.

Can You Believe It?

"Love has been perfected among us in this: that we may have boldness in the day of judgment; because as He is, so are we in this world."
– 1 John 4:17

We are in His place now! When God looks at us, He cannot help but see His Son. This is the true essence of righteousness. Every part of our old self is dead, including yesterday's mistakes and failures. Jesus traded His standing with the Father for ours, and now we can live, relate, and worship like He would. Some would call that arrogance, but it is true humility. You must be humble in order to admit that, despite your best efforts, you are unable to be righteous on your own. And, in that place, God's grace comes to make you new, to clothe you in righteousness, and to welcome you home.

"Yet indeed I also count all things loss for the excellence of the knowledge of Christ Jesus my Lord... that I may gain Christ and be found in Him, not having my own righteousness, which is from the law, but that which is through faith in Christ, the righteousness which is from God by faith."
– Philippians 3:8-9

What we believe is what will manifest. What you think about comes about. Your thoughts are the preview of your life's coming attractions. However, the righteousness of Christ is only obtainable by faith. If you do not know, understand, and believe you are in right standing with God, then it will never be your experience, even if it is true. Many people put more faith in Adam's ability to keep us unrighteous sinners than Jesus' ability to make us righteous saints.

It is true that sin separated us from God, and our nature was evil. However, we cannot allow who we *were* to prevent us from standing firm in who we *are*. How disappointing would it be to receive an incredible gift and never use it? The life, identity, and commission we have is a costly possession. What are we doing with it? It's time to share with the world that sin has been defeated, and a new life awaits anyone who will receive Jesus as their Lord, Savior, and righteousness. There is no more separation from God for all who believe.

Knowing that to be true, it will help to understand that this is why Paul was persecuted so heavily. It was not because he believed in Jesus, but because he preached a message of righteousness apart from works—something very offensive and counter-cultural. First-century Jews could not stand to see their holy God treat sinners with love, compassion, and mercy because they saw it as unfair, especially compared to their strict, "devout," and self-righteous lifestyles. However, in reality, it was the most legally fair treatment available. The connection point is the Cross. Jesus' death was the just judgment for our sins. There is nothing remaining that needs to be paid for. The debt is canceled. We are free to leave our old selves behind and to be Jesus to this world. Believing in the power of this Gospel is the only way we will ever live in what Jesus paid for.

The Cross Means Something Today

The resurrection of Jesus is not just a promise of getting a ticket to heaven. It is proof that God's resurrection power is available and active today for any who would access it. Let me lay it out like this: Adam's choice to eat from the tree introduced sin, sickness, and death into the world. Jesus, the "second Adam," through His obedience to God by His own "tree," the Cross, restored righteousness, healing, and life to all who believe.

There is nothing that is lacking anymore! The wait for restoration is over! The wait for healing or right-standing with God is over! The wait for a satisfying life is over! Jesus purchased everything necessary, not only for eternal life as we understand it, but also for eternal life beginning *now*! As 2 Peter 1:3 says, "His divine power has given to us all things that pertain to life and godliness." That means right now, we lack nothing and have everything we need to live out God's call for our lives.

This has massive implications to our lives today because it removes all limitations. It means we no longer need to be victims of unsatisfactory circumstances. Our age, strengths, opportunities, position, or anything else can never again limit our ability to live a godly life representing Christ. So many people wait for either the right time, the right feeling, or the right behavior before ever considering that God wants to use them! Even worse is the belief that the end goal of Christianity is just to live a moral life, die, and go to heaven.

It is vital that you understand Jesus' death and resurrection is more than a religious or historical event—it is the beginning of your new life. Remember that you were crucified *with* Christ, and because of this co-crucifixion, you were co-buried. This finally puts us in the position to be co-raised with Him—"the life which I now live in the flesh I live by faith in the Son of God who loved me and gave Himself for me" (Gal. 2:20).

"Therefore, if anyone is in Christ, he is a new creation; old things have passed away; behold, all things have become new."
– 2 Corinthians 5:17

This resurrected life is brand new, and it is completely different from the old life. Because of this, we are free from anything that bound the old man. The chains of sin and death were buried with Christ, and in their place is a robe of righteousness and a crown of life. This is where the term "born again" comes from. Why would the authors of Scripture use this term if we were not given a new life, a new beginning, and a new birth?

When we see that we are totally new and not who we used to be, our lives become legitimate representations of Christ. We finally believe that the truth sets us free. We are not bound by our beliefs, and we are free to minister from a place of grace. The power behind our actions is Christ in us, His Holy Spirit, and His divine ability working through our lives.

There is no more condemnation for any of our past mistakes, failures, or sins (see Rom. 8:1). You are holy, blameless, and above reproach in God's sight (see Col. 1:22). God has adopted you into His family as one of His own (see 1 John 3:1). Now that we are fully loved, filled with His Spirit, and commissioned by His Son, we are His manifestation of love on the earth to bring the reality of His Kingdom into reach. We have the benefits of righteousness, healing, and life. The curse Adam initiated into the world has been undone. Anything that comes from sin and death has been eliminated, and the sons and daughters of God have been made the authority on this earth.

The only way to walk in this is to simply believe Christ has done it all. The requirement of the law has been met in Christ. The beauty of this gift of God is not just our freedom from the punishment we deserved, but also the empowerment grace brings to all who receive it. The new command we have is to love as we have been loved. If the Body of Christ can walk that command out, we will grow in the influence that comes through loving like Jesus.

Chapter Seven

Slaves to Righteousness

This book is not about your problems or the strongholds of the devil in your life. This is not a book about sin and correcting wrong behavior, although I hope that beliefs and behaviors are changed as you take hold of what you're reading. One of my goals has always been and will always be to help the Body of Christ come to one realization: the truth of Her righteous identity. The revelation in this book on the three giants is really a revelation of righteousness. If you believed you were truly righteous from the inside out, you would not feel condemned, you would not fear punishment, and you would not hide behind a mask and live in pride.

You cannot be prideful when you receive God's righteousness by faith in Jesus. You cannot be fearful when you know you are righteous, because you are assured that God is your protector, your provider, and your promise-keeper. You cannot be condemned when you know you are righteous because Jesus is your propitiation. The word propitiation simply means satisfaction of wrath or atonement. What Jesus did at the Cross on your behalf satisfied God. He is no longer angry with you. God sees you as He sees His Son.

Under the Old Covenant, when a sacrifice was brought to the tabernacle or temple, the Levitical priests would inspect the sacrifice, most commonly a lamb, in order to ensure that it was spotless and without blemish. Notice that they would look at the *sacrifice,* not the *sinner*! Now when we come to worship, God does not look at us, even if we have made a mistake. He looks at the sacrifice made on our behalf, and we have the *most* spotless lamb as our substitute. God is not looking at your sin anymore, and He is not inspecting you for any faults. He is looking at His Son's sacrifice! There is no need to be afraid, hide your sin, or feel condemned. He has taken your place.

Beyond forgiveness, Jesus offers a new life! This new life comes with a new nature. That means that no matter what you do, you are still righteous. No matter how many times you miss the mark, God's love and acceptance of you is still 100%. This scandalous truth is the power of grace. It is not punishment or expectations of a good performance that produce the right behaviors. It is grace, God's unmerited, unearned favor and ability, that works inside of you and empowers you to do what He has commanded.

Under grace, you have been set free from the law which means you have equally been set free from the burden of condemnation, the pressure of fear, and the motive of pride. Under grace, sin has no more power over you. Many of us think of sin as an action, a wrong behavior. We commonly think and speak in terms of the verb "to sin."

If I say "sin," most Christians would think of lying, stealing, cheating, looking at pornography, etc. We think of "sin" as an action verb. However, in Scripture, we see a different message when we study the use of the word "sin." Paul used the word "sin" 55 times as he wrote the book of Romans. Did you know that 48 of the times the word "sin" is mentioned it's not a verb but a *noun* (the Greek word *harmartia*)? Only seven times in the entire book of Romans is the word "sin" actually a verb (*hamartan*). For example, Romans 6:15 says, "What then? Shall we *sin* because we are not under law but under grace?"

A verb is an *action*, but a noun is defined as a *person, place,* or *thing*. Nearly every time we see Paul writing about sin, he is referencing the position of sin! Why is this so significant? Because, when you understand that sin is more often referred to as a place or thing rather than a bad behavior, you will find the secret to freedom. And it's right in the text!

"...our old man was crucified with Him,
that the body of sin might be done away with,
that we should no longer be slaves of sin. "
– Romans 6:6

The wording in the book of Romans communicates as if sin were a *place*. Different translations say that you were "a prisoner of sin," and that you were "in a prison of sin." Those are all true descriptions. Without Jesus, you are stuck in an inescapable cage of sinfulness. Sadly, this is where many Christians live their lives. They are stuck in a jail cell with an open door.

Now that Jesus has died on the Cross, you have the opportunity to live by faith in Him, which transfers you into a prison of righteousness! This is the best prison exchange program in existence. You are now a prisoner of righteousness! You were in a prison of sin, enslaved to sin. Then, by faith, you were saved, born again, and transformed into a new creation in Christ. You now have a new heart and a new nature. Congratulations, you are now a slave to righteousness, and that is a glorious place to be! I have even more good news: in this new prison, you are trapped.

What is funny is that you cannot get out, even if you tried. So many believers are trying to perform, trying to do good enough, and trying not to sin. They are attempting to fix themselves and their "sinful natures." However, if they are in Christ, they cannot get out of righteousness! They have already become righteous, bound to righteousness by a blood covenant. Righteousness is as ingrained in them as their own DNA.

"And having been set free from sin, you became slaves of righteousness."
– Romans 6:18

Just as you were trapped under the power of sin (the noun), you are now under the power and dominion of Christ's righteousness. Let me show it to you more clearly. Did you do any "good" works before you met Jesus? Think back before you were saved. Can you actually think of some good things you accomplished or helped with while you were still a sinner? What did you do? You may have helped your parents or told the truth. You might have given some change to a homeless person. You may have helped someone cross the street or volunteered some of your time to charity.

Nevertheless, despite all those "good" works, you were still stuck in your own sinfulness. No matter how hard you tried, how much good you did, or how helpful you made yourself, you were *trapped* in the prison of sin. Nothing you did could get you out. All the good stuff you did (your serving, giving, helping, volunteering) meant nothing. Did any of your good works get you out of this prison of sin? No!

Therefore, if none of your good works could get you out of the prison of sin, then why do you think that your bad works, sins, and shortcomings can take you out of the prison of righteousness? We are *slaves* to righteousness! We are trapped in a prison of righteousness, a prison of right-standing with

God! Our bad deeds do not have any more power to pull us out of righteousness than our good deeds had to pull us out of sin.

Do you realize how significant this truth is? This will set you free if you believe it! The problem is that most people believe more in the power of sin than the power of righteousness. They believe more in the feelings of condemnation than the truth of the Gospel. If you know that your good deeds cannot pull you out of the prison of sin, but you believe your bad deeds can pull you out of the prison of righteousness, ultimately you are saying that Adam's sin in the garden was greater than Jesus' sacrifice on the cross.

This one misconception could keep you in bondage for the rest of your life. Everything comes back to what you believe. You can be a Christian who is in legal, right-standing with God and still believe that you are unworthy and separated from God. By believing this, you have given the enemy the right to torment you because you have partnered with his lies. However, if you believe that no matter what you do, you have been put into right relationship with God, you will begin to experience and manifest righteousness!

"But now having been set free from sin, and having become slaves of God, you have your fruit to holiness, and the end, everlasting life."
– Romans 6:22

The idea that you are stuck in sin until you behave better is a lie from the pit of hell! It is equally twisted to believe that your relationship with God depends on your performance instead of Christ's. You are in a prison of righteousness, and you can do nothing to change that. You have been bought with a price. It's no longer you who live but Christ who lives in you.

No more condemnation. No more fear. No more pride. No more guilt. No more shame. No more living in the past. No more living under the law. This is the power of the Cross! He literally exchanged everything for you! Your life is His and His life is now yours. This includes everything He has. His relationship with the Father, His righteousness, His peace, His power, and His nature are all yours right now!

"But where sin abounded, grace abounded much more... What shall we say then? Shall we continue in sin that grace may abound? Certainly not! How shall we who died to sin live any longer in it?"
– Romans 5:20, 6:1-2

To be very clear, living in the prison of righteousness does not give you a license to sin. Even Paul makes sure to state this twice in that same chapter. God's grace changes your heart because you were not even designed for sin. If you think that you can now sin freely without punishment or repercussions, you need a deeper revelation of the Cross. Jesus' perfect sacrifice is not something to be trampled on.

If you are considering living in sin while enjoying the benefits of forgiveness and grace, I pray that the Lord gives you an even clearer view of His holiness and His purity. Keeping this tension in mind is a key to remaining in balance. God is great and mighty, someone to be feared and respected, but He is also loving and merciful, someone who leaves the ninety-nine to go after the one.

Abusing grace is not grace at all. It is deliberate, willful sin, and that is not His plan for your life. He has set you free from the prison of sin, calling you higher as a partaker of His divine nature. His ambition is that you would be conformed to the image of His Son. We are the manifest sons and daughters of God the earth is "earnestly expecting" to see revealed (see Rom. 8:19)! His design was not just to give you a life where you are not sinning but to call you into a life where you are being transformed into the image of His Son.

The Church has become too familiar with the phrase, "There's grace for that." This has become the motto for those who are trying to excuse their sin rather than be set free from it. It's true: there is grace. But if you were actually receiving it, your life would be transformed! Being trapped in sin is evidence of being under the law—not under grace. When your cycles and destructive habits begin to break, this is the sign of true grace! Embrace this revelation with an open and true heart, and your life will be changed.

As you move forward, even more free from fear, pride, and condemnation, I want you to see something clearly. All of these areas of bondage are the result of sin. Condemnation is only present because of the law which reveals mankind's inability to measure up (sin). The fear of punishment is only present where punishment is deserved (sin). Pride is often covering up for insecurity and inadequacy, caused by an awareness of brokenness or flaws (sin). How is sin defeated? Most people immediately think "the Cross." That is true, but practically speaking, how did the Cross remove the power of sin from our lives?

"The sting of death is sin, and the strength of sin is the law. But thanks be to God, who gives us the victory through our Lord Jesus Christ."
—1 Corinthians 15:56-57

The secret power of sin is wrapped up in the law. Read that verse again: "the strength of sin is the *law*!" The entire Old Covenant method of measuring your standing with God by your actions and ability to be "good enough" is what gives sin its strength. As long as you believe your connection with God rises and falls on your behavior, you are giving place to sin. As long as you are trying to earn your righteousness, you are feeding sin and giving it more strength in your life because you will never be able to measure up on your own. It will only reveal your inability, and thus, throw you into the cycle of sin, condemnation, and failure. You feel condemned because you don't meet God's standard. So you try harder, but you fail. Then after failing repeatedly, you resort to sin and compromise for comfort. This lifestyle only leaves you with more condemnation.

When you come out from under the law and come under the New Covenant freedom of grace, you are accepted, beloved, and chosen because of who Christ is. You are forever in right-standing with God, and sin has now lost its strength. You have been given the victory! Because God's love is unconditional in the face of your shortcomings, you are free to experience His affection at all times. "The goodness of God leads you to repentance" when you fail (Rom. 2:4). This is where grace flows in because you have humbled yourself. "God gives grace to the humble" (James 4:6). You are allowing His "strength to be made perfect" in your weakness (2 Cor. 12:9). You begin to thrive and live as a son or daughter of God.

Sin has lost its strength because you are righteous, redeemed, and repositioned under grace, not the law! As a slave to righteousness, you are His, and there is nothing separating you now. As long as you continue to live your life surrendered to Him, you cannot escape His power and His grace that transforms you more and more into His image.

"It is for freedom that Christ has set us free. Stand firm, then, and do not let yourselves be burdened again by a yoke of slavery."
– Galatians 5:1 NIV

Paul was serious about this topic of being set free from the law of sin and death. He had lived as a slave to the same law, trying to measure up to its standards, but all it produced was a cycle of sin and striving (see Rom. 7:14-24). He was zealously correcting the Galatian church because some of its members were being pulled away by the belief that righteousness was not obtained through faith but through following the law.

You can hear his heart through that verse: "do not let yourselves be burdened again." Paul was asking, "If you have freedom now, why would you go back?" People were lifting the Law of Moses higher than the "perfect law of liberty," the law of Christ (James 1:25). Paul wanted the attention of the Galatian church to be on Christ, who was crucified not only *for* them but *as* them (see Gal. 2:20). Paul wanted them to see that Jesus came for one goal and that was to atone for the sins of man in order to set them free from themselves. He came to bring freedom from every curse of sin, which is the byproduct of Adam's fall.

The motivation of Jesus is beautiful because this freedom comes with no strings attached. He wants to set you free so that you can experience freedom! "It was for freedom that Christ set us free..." (Gal. 5:1 NASB). He *is* freedom. Living in Him is the most free you will ever be. True freedom is not the ability to do whatever you "feel" like doing. It is the ability to choose one thing in the midst of hundreds of other options. True freedom is possessing the power to say no to sin, temptation, and compromise, choosing not to engage whenever it attempts to lure you. Instead, you have the option to choose selflessness and love toward others. Freedom is powerful. Freedom is responsible. Freedom looks and acts like Jesus.

Who He Is = Who You Are

You are now free. As a new creation and partaker of the divine nature, you have been made one with God in perfect unity (see 2 Peter 1:4). You were co-crucified, co-buried, and co-resurrected with Christ. You are free to enjoy the relationship with God that is available now as you are co-seated in heavenly places. Nothing can touch you, and the only task left for you to do is believe. Do you believe that you are not under the law anymore? Do you believe that God's love and forgiveness for you are stronger than your sin and rebellion? Do you believe that you are now in Jesus' place and viewed by the Father through His perfect sacrifice?

If your answers are yes, you have great reason to celebrate. You are believing the Word! You have already begun to renew your mind with truth, which is the source of all transformation. You are not under condemnation because your righteousness does not come from your behavior. You are not enslaved to fear because your life is not even your own anymore. It is God's, and He has sworn that He will take good care of His children. You are not under the influence of pride anymore. Your significance has no attachment to your achievements, accomplishments, or actions. You have been delivered from "self" altogether, and now every part of your identity stems from Him.

When you see that your life is completely wrapped up in Jesus, you have no more need to keep your eyes on yourself. The goal all along was to get you to see that the freedom you seek has already been paid for and offered to you. My prayer is that, when you set this book down, you are not simply motivated to "do better." I pray you are driven to spend time in God's Word, fix your thoughts on the Gospel, fill yourself with truth, and renew your mind more than ever. Freedom from fear, pride, or condemnation is not the focus. The focus is Christ. Embrace His finished work, experience His love, and own your identity as a beloved son or daughter!

It is my highest privilege to share these truths with you. The liberty has already been given, but it needs to be proclaimed. This freedom we now have needs to be shouted from the rooftops (see Is. 61:1)! The Spirit of the Lord came upon Jesus to preach good tidings to the poor. He healed the brokenhearted. He proclaimed liberty to the captives.

"Therefore if the Son makes you free, you shall be free indeed."
—John 8:36

You are free indeed because the Son has set you free. Never again will you have to be a victim of the byproducts of sin, and that includes fear, pride, and condemnation. You have the limitless love of God overflowing inside of you, never to be stopped. You are spotless because the Spotless Lamb covered you with His righteousness. You can now rest in godly humility because your confidence is in God and not yourself.

Conclusion

I pray that as you continue your walk with the Lord, He would strengthen you with His Word, comfort you with His love, and lead you with His Spirit. I firmly believe that the Church is rising up and believing who God says She is. You are a part of this great awakening. You are the manifestation of Jesus on this earth. Refuse to listen to any other voice, and follow His. You know the voice of the Good Shepherd because you are His sheep (see John 10:27). He is always taking you higher and leading you beside quiet waters into the land of the living!

He truly is your Savior and Friend, and He desires more than anything that you be swept up into relationship with Him all the days of your life. Freedom is far less of a destination and far more of a reality you choose to live in by walking in an intimate and daily relationship with the Lord. Know that you have received an abundance of grace. Know that you have received the gift of righteousness. Know that you have the capability to reign in life. Now, the only choice remaining is: will you believe it?

Salvation

I don't want to end this book without giving everyone an opportunity to accept Christ as their Lord and Savior. If you've already made this decision, I'm grateful and would love to hear your feedback and experience of *It is Finished.*

If you haven't made this decision before, I would like to extend an invitation. The reality of the finished work of the Cross is yours to experience right where you are. You don't need to run to an altar. The altar is in your heart. The application of this book will take on new life and new form after you allow the blood of Jesus to wash over you, cleanse you, and make you a completely new creation.

If you want to experience the victorious life of a son or daughter of God and be welcomed into the family of heaven, open your mouth and say this prayer with me:

Dear God, I come to you now with my heart wide open. I can't live any longer without knowing You. I'm not here to take up a religion but to enter a relationship. I want to know You as my Maker, my Lord, and my Savior. I want to call You my Father.

I've lived a life that has served me, myself, and I. I've hurt people, I've fallen short, and I've sinned more than I can recount. I need Your mercy and Your forgiveness. Will You remove my sins far from me and make me Your own? Will You repay the people I've trespassed against and stolen from? I cannot possibly pay for the sum of my sins, but you can and already did.

I give You my heart. I believe in You, Jesus. I accept Your death, burial, and resurrection as my own. You took my place on the Cross, and for that I am eternally grateful. I surrender to Your Lordship and I commit to give You my life, just as You gave me Yours. Come into my heart, deliver me, heal me, and make me completely new. I want the fullness of your salvation now... a salvation that removes darkness, cleanses my past, and awakens me into a new life! I clothe myself in Your righteousness! I accept You, Jesus Christ, as my new identity! Holy Spirit, come and baptize me. Come and manifest the supernatural power and love of Jesus Christ in and through me!

Amen.

Welcome to the family! If you prayed this prayer, we want to hear from you!

Please email us at testimonies@graceplaceredding.com so we can keep in touch with you and encourage you in your walk with Jesus!

On our website, you can find additional resources on identity and discipleship—all of which are there to help you in your journey with Christ.

You go to www.graceplacemedia.com on your browser or scan the QR code below with your smartphone.

About Grace Place

Grace Place Ministries is a discipleship community fueled by a passion to see God's people walk out their identity in Christ and establish His Kingdom upon the earth. We are committed to developing mature Christian leaders through one-on-one mentoring, building family through weekly gatherings, and providing leadership opportunities designed to facilitate connection and growth. We travel frequently to minister around the world and create resources to build up the Church in her righteous identity.

Vision

Mature sons and daughters
established in their identity in Christ,
spreading the Gospel of grace and truth.

Mission

Disciple young adults.
Minister around the world.
Resource the nations.

Discipleship is our Mission; Will you Join Us?

Now, more than ever, the body of Christ needs to arise and shine. The world is searching for answers and is in need of an encounter with God's love and truth. Who will raise up a generation to bring answers our world is desperately seeking?

"For the earnest expectation of the creation eagerly waits for the revealing of the sons of God."
– Romans 8:19

Whether it is a young man or woman needing a mentor or an entire church seeking the resources to disciple their community, you can make an impact!

Become a Partner with Grace Place Ministries:

Go to:

WWW.GRACEPLACEPARTNER.COM

Additional Resources

The Lost Art of Discipleship

God's Model for Transforming the World

Discipleship is not a man-made idea. It is God's design for world transformation. *The Lost Art of Discipleship* is the uncovering of heaven's blueprints for remodeling the kingdoms of the earth into the Kingdom of our God. In his cornerstone book, Daniel Newton pulls from 20 years of experience in discipleship. As you read, prepare your heart to be ignited with the fires of revival that once swept the globe as in the days of the Early Church. It is time for the people of God to arise and shine for our light has come!

Additional Resources

The Lost Art of Discipleship
Workbook

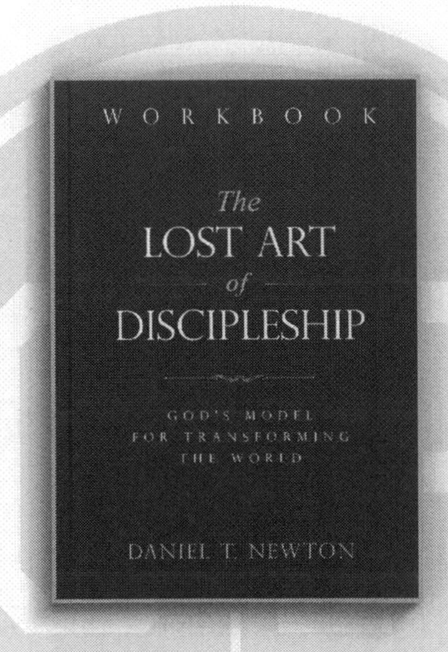

Enrich your understanding and increase your mastery of God's model for world transformation. This companion workbook to *The Lost Art of Discipleship* book is filled with exclusive content, in-depth exercises, and practical coaching to introduce a lifestyle of discipleship in your day-to-day walk. Whether you have been following the Lord for years or recently surrendered your life to Jesus, this manual breaks down the Great Commission and equips you for a life of fruitfulness!

Additional Resources

The Lost Art of Discipleship

Online Course

You can live the Great Commission. Every believer is called to embrace Jesus' final command: to make disciples... and this interactive online course is designed to take you even deeper into the rich content taught in *The Lost Art of Discipleship*.

Whether you are wanting to position yourself as a son or daughter, lead as a father or mother, or create a culture of discipleship, this course is for you! Rediscover the lost art with over five hours of video content, practical teaching, quizzes, and supernatural activations from Daniel Newton.

Available at www.GracePlaceMedia.com

@GracePlaceDiscipleship

Additional Resources

Immeasurable

Reviewing the Goodness of God

You are made in the image of the Miracle Worker, designed to manifest His glorious nature. *Immeasurable: Reviewing the Goodness of God* is a collection of 100 real-life stories of salvation, healing, deliverance, signs and wonders, reconciliation, and provision. Every miracle is a prophetic declaration of what God wants to do in, through, and for someone just like you.

Additional Resources

Truth in Tension
55 Days to
Living in Balance

Never Give Up
The Supernatural Power of
Christ-like Endurance

Other Titles

The Lost Art of Perseverance
Rediscover God's Perspective on Your Trials

All Things
Have Become New, Work Together for Good, Are Possible

Additional Resources

GP Music: Beginnings

Everyone has a story. Most people don't realize that God doesn't just want to improve their story. He wants to rewrite it. Beginnings offers a fresh start, a new focus. This worship album invites you into the core anthems of grace and truth which have impacted us at Grace Place.

Our prayer is that this album helps you lay down your past mistakes, your present circumstances, and your future worries in order to lift both hands high in surrender to the One you were created to worship. We ask that you join us in a new beginning — an exciting start to a life filled with perseverance, focus, and surrender.

KEEP US UPDATED

We would love to connect with you and hear about everything God has done in your life while reading this book! We also would love to hear how we can be praying for you. Submit a testimony or prayer request by going to www.GracePlaceRedding.com/mytestimony

STAY CONNECTED WITH GRACE PLACE

Are you interested in staying up to date with Grace Place Ministries and receiving encouraging resources via email?

Visit our website:
www.GracePlaceRedding.com

Sign up for our newsletter at:
www.GracePlaceRedding.com/newsletter

Follow us on social media:
@GracePlaceDiscipleship

Made in the USA
Las Vegas, NV
04 January 2023